Pr...
Goo...

"*Goodbye, Sweet Girl* is heartb... ...d urgently truthful in its harrowing and tender examination of when empathy fails—and when it wins." —*Los Angeles Review*

"Kelly Sundberg's lyrical, devastating 2014 essay about domestic violence, 'It Will Look Like a Sunset,' made readers hold their collective breath. It's now expanded into a full-length memoir about Sundberg's husband, a man who was wonderful and violent at turns."
—*Elle*, "The 30 Best Books to Read This Summer"

"*Goodbye, Sweet Girl*, bursting with such heartfelt, beautifully crafted scenes, is a gift for those who've experienced the pain of growing up and out of abusive relationships and a guide for those who seek insight and understanding." —*New York Journal of Books*

"In this can't-take-your-eyes-off-the-page memoir, hard-bitten Idaho is a savage landscape 'full of sawed-off mountains,' nuclear waste, and wild animals just outside your door. But for Sundberg, the real danger shares her bed. How does a violent partner erode the terrain of your heart? And are you ever too old to run away from home?"
—*O, The Oprah Magazine*, "Top Books of Summer"

"*Goodbye, Sweet Girl* is a beautiful, devastating, and nuanced story of domestic abuse and escape that does true justice to the experiences of the victims without judgment or criticism of their choices."
—*Bustle*

"Because of its subject matter, *Goodbye, Sweet Girl* might seem difficult to read, but Sundberg's crystalline prose and insightful narration lighten the reading experience. . . . [Her] story is haunting, propulsive, and, perhaps for some readers, familiar. Her wrenching memoir deserves to be read by a wide audience so that we can all learn to recognize the signs of domestic abuse." —*BookPage*

"Mesmerizing and poetic, *Goodbye, Sweet Girl* is a harrowing, cautionary, and ultimately redemptive tale that brilliantly illuminates one woman's transformation." —Bookreporter.com

"Kelly Sundberg gives one of the most brave and beautifully written accounts of a marriage gone wrong in her memoir, *Goodbye, Sweet Girl*. Sundberg looks at both the tenderness and the violence of her abusive marriage, while also analyzing why women remain too long in dangerous relationships." —*Brooklyn Digest*

"[*Goodbye, Sweet Girl* helps us] to better understand each of our nuances and complexities, how any of us rationalizes our decisions, and how we find the courage to take care of ourselves and to speak our truths. . . . [Sundberg writes] her truth with a deep sense of compassion." —themillions.com

"*Goodbye, Sweet Girl* is a story of domestic violence and survival, written by Kelly Sundberg, who experienced abuse at the hands of her husband. A strong and empowering memoir, the layers of Sundberg's life are utterly inspiring."

—Women.com, "15 Awesome Books with Strong Female Protagonists"

"Reading Kelly Sundberg's writing—fresh, luminous, spirited—is a pleasure second only to witnessing her decision to survive. *Goodbye, Sweet Girl* is a meditation on what it takes to save your own life."

—Ariel Levy, author of *The Rules Do Not Apply*

"It is a hell of a thing to write about brutality and suffering with strength, grace, generosity, and beauty. That's precisely what Kelly Sundberg has done in her gripping memoir about marriage and domestic violence. Sundberg's honesty is astonishing, how she laid so much of herself bare, how she did not demonize a man who deserves to be demonized. Instead, she offers a portrait of a broken man and a broken marriage and an abiding love, what it took to set herself free from it all. In shimmering, openhearted prose, she shows that it took everything."

—Roxane Gay, *New York Times* bestselling author
of *Hunger* and *Bad Feminist*

"*Goodbye, Sweet Girl* is a breathtaking gut punch of a memoir. Real talk: the story is hard. We spend so much time pretending that domestic violence doesn't exist. We spend so much time doubting women. Enough. Sundberg gives us the truth in all its complexity; fear and hope and fury in gorgeous, near-cinematic prose that made me weep, and cheer, and understand. Here is how we save ourselves. Here is how we survive."

—Megan Stielstra, author of *The Wrong Way to Save Your Life*

"In her stunning memoir, Kelly Sundberg examines the heartbreaking bonds of love, detailing her near decade-long marriage's slide into horrific abuse. Sundberg shares her own confusions, fears, and empathy for her violent husband, even as she comes to realize he will never change. This is an immensely courageous story that will break your heart, leave you in tears, and, finally, offer hope and redemption. Brava, Kelly Sundberg." —Rene Denfeld, author of *The Child Finder*

"A fierce, frightening, soulful reckoning—*Goodbye, Sweet Girl* is an expertly rendered memoir that investigates why we stay in relationships that hurt us, and how we survive when we leave them. Kelly

Sundberg is a force. She has written the rare book that has the power to change lives."—Christa Parravani, author of *Her: A Memoir*

"With disorienting elegance Kelly Sundberg shows her readers how difficult it can be to believe even your own experiences of abuse when they begin in what seems to be a loving relationship, and unfold alongside depression and confusion arising as a result of that very abuse—and perhaps worst of all, when in the midst of such doubt, fear, and sorrow, loved ones question your judgment. Kelly brings clear eyes, an open heart, and the vulnerability that comes from long healing to a story of domestic grief and horrific abuse. . . . This is an important bock." —Bonnie Nadzam, author of *Lamb* and *Lions*

"A shattering of the silence that enables domestic violence to continue, *Goodbye, Sweet Girl* shines a fierce light on how complex and sometimes joyous a relationship that's also an abusive cage can be, why women gradually lose the orientation they need to find the exit, and how they escape when they do, or how this one did. This book is a testament—and a warning to batterers that the silence is broken, and their secrets are leaking out."

—Rebecca Solnit, author of *Call Them by Their True Names: American Crises (and Essays)*

"In this powerful debut memoir, Sundberg delivers a harrowing account of an abusive marriage and how she left it. . . . Sundberg cogently ties together the painful chain of events in her life and the personal growth that resulted from it."—*Publishers Weekly*

"Lyrical and taut, *Goodbye, Sweet Girl* provides readers with an honest and critical account of partner violence."—*Booklist* (starred review)

Goodbye, Sweet Girl

A Story of Domestic Violence and Survival

KELLY SUNDBERG

HARPER ● PERENNIAL

NEW YORK ● LONDON ● TORONTO ● SYDNEY ● NEW DELHI ● AUCKLAND

HARPER ● PERENNIAL

A hardcover edition of this book was published in 2018 by HarperCollins Publishers.

The events and experiences that I write about are all true and have been faithfully rendered as I remember them. In some places, I've changed the names, identities, and other specifics of individuals who have played a role in my life in order to protect their privacy. The conversations I re-create come from my clear recollections of them, though they are not written to represent word-for-word transcripts. In all instances, I've retold them in a way that evokes the feeling and meaning of what was said, always keeping with the true essence of the exchanges.

Material adapted from "It Will Look Like a Sunset," originally published by *Guernica*, April 2014.

Grateful acknowledgment is made to Nick Flynn for permission to reprint lines from "forgetting something," copyright © 2011 by Nick Flynn. Reprinted from *The Captain Asks for a Show of Hands* and used with permission of the author and Graywolf Press. All rights reserved.

HarperCollins books may be purchased for educational, business, or sales promotional use. For information, please email the Special Markets Department at SPsales@harpercollins.com.

FIRST HARPER PERENNIAL EDITION PUBLISHED 2019.

Designed by Bonni Leon-Berman

Library of Congress Cataloging-in-Publication Data has been applied for.

ISBN 978-0-06-249768-0 (pbk.)

19 20 21 22 23 LSC 10 9 8 7 6 5 4 3 2 1

For Megan, Kelly M., and Rebecca:

The women who opened the window.

First thing we should do

if we ever meet again

is make a cage of our bodies where we can place

whatever still shines

—NICK FLYNN, "FORGETTING SOMETHING"

Contents

Goodbye, Sweet Girl

Prologue

IN A TOWN built on a hill, in a state full of sawed-off mountains where muddy roads curved along polluted streams, metal deposits in the water gleamed like steely rainbows, and the muted sunlight filtered through shadowy trees, lived an archivist. His was a job of remembrance.

Mine was a job of forgetting.

On his phone my husband, Caleb, the archivist, had a collection of self-portraits. Each looked the same, with only variations in his clothing, his facial hair, or the background. In one of the portraits he stood in front of our bookshelf in a plaid collared shirt, unrelenting eyes staring firmly into the camera and his long but neatly trimmed beard masking a frown. In another he sat on the couch in front of the living room window. He wore a blue hooded sweatshirt this time, and his face was clean-shaven, but the expression was the same. Unrelenting. Impenetrable.

At night, as we cuddled on the couch, my head on his shoulder, a blanket draped over our legs, he would scroll through the dozens of photos. "Why do you take all of these?" I teased him.

"I'm pretending they're my author photo," he said. "I want to look serious."

This behavior seemed strange to me, but he often had

inexplicable behaviors. I laughed, grabbed the phone, scrolled through the lot. "They look more like mug shots," I said, tossing it back in his lap.

Later, he told me the truth. He took the photos as documentation. He took the photos to document his misery. And his shame.

IN MORGANTOWN, THE West Virginia college town where we lived, there was a twelve-story dorm named Summit Hall: a sterile box of metal and windows. Within that box, eighteen- to twenty-two-year-olds got high, lost their virginity, studied for exams, cried to their mothers out of homesickness, slept through the long days, and partied through the short nights. They did these things in rooms stacked on top of each other, in a contained mess of excitement, experimentation, joy, and loss.

Underneath all of these rooms, on the first floor, was an apartment—a beautiful cage—with polished wood floors, chrome pendant lights, and leather furniture. It was an apartment designed for a faculty family, the "resident faculty leaders," or, as I liked to call us, "Dorm Mom and Dad." It was the apartment where I had lived for only four months with my husband of eight years, Caleb, and our seven-year-old son, Reed. It was the apartment where my husband and I made love quietly, hoping not to be overheard by the girls who lived on the floor above us. It was the apartment where I tucked our little boy into his bed, wrapped his blanket around his shoulders, said, "I love you, buddy." He mur-

mured, "I love you too," shutting his eyes against the dark night.

I closed the door to his room and went to find Caleb in the next room. Leaning into his chest, I said, "I love you too." He looked down at me, smiled, and kissed me.

Our son was so proud to be living in the dorm. None of his friends got to walk into a building full of college students who doted on them. Everyone who met our son—a sweet, intelligent, and funny boy with a superhero obsession—fell in love with him, and the college students were no exception. At his birthday party, he was lavished with presents: Pokémon cards from the eighteen-year-old boys, who still loved Pokémon themselves, and board games from the girls, who all wanted to come to the apartment and play with him.

At school, when he had to draw a picture of his home, even though we had spent most of his childhood in a small house on the other side of town, he drew a picture of the dorm. He drew a tall rectangle filled with square windows. In front of the building stood Reed, Caleb, our two dogs, and me. At the bottom of the page, he wrote "Welcome to Summit Hall!" We are all smiling, even the dogs.

ON THE DAY of Reed's party, I pinned a blue ribbon to his costume that read "Birthday Boy!" I decorated the apartment with streamers, confetti, and a circus-style popcorn machine. I put out red-and-white movie-style cartons for the popcorn, baked a dozen birthday cupcakes, filled bowls with various kinds of candy for decorating, and placed clues all over the dormitory for a massive, building-wide scavenger hunt for the kids.

In the morning, even though I still had all of these things to do, I didn't want the day to start. I could tell it was going to be a bad one. I dressed slowly, not wanting to leave the safety of my bedroom, but unable to remain there. We had spent the night before cleaning the apartment, but I still needed to clean the main bathroom. I poured myself a cup of coffee, then moved to the bathroom and started scrubbing the counters quickly. Caleb came and stood in the doorway. His eyes on me. I didn't look at him. Just kept scrubbing.

"Can you bring me the toilet brush from the other bathroom?" I said, without looking up.

He left, returned with the toilet brush, kneeled down by the toilet, and started scrubbing, moving the brush back and forth in angry movements.

"You don't need to do that," I said. "Just leave it there. I'll get it."

He took the brush and threw it against the wall, splashing toilet water all over the floor. I flinched. The dogs, who usually followed us from room to room, crept out into our son's room. Caleb turned to me and screamed, "I knew you were going to do this! The apartment is fine as is. It's never enough for you."

I put down my sponge and ran out of the room. I knew what was coming. My counselor had told me to "exit the situation" when he was like that. I grabbed my keys and phone, but he chased me, yanked my phone out of my hand, and threw it against the wall, shattering it. It was one of many phones he had broken in the previous year. I still had the keys in my hand. I eyed the door. He saw me. If I could get out the door, I could make a run for it. The dorm was closed for Thanksgiving break, but three of the resident assistants were at the front desk until noon. He would never hit me in front of them.

I eyed the door again, tried to step around him. Caleb moved in front of me, stretching his arms out wide. Then I did it. I ducked under his arm, opened the door, and ran as fast as I could to safety.

Except that he had followed me. He had followed me, even though the resident assistants were there. They stood at the desk, smiled when they saw me, and then paused, faces frozen. I raced by as he chased me. "Come back here!" he yelled. "Come back, you fucking bitch."

I cried out "Call the police!" to the resident assistants, then thought, Oh my God, did I really say that? Did I just say that?

They stared. "Really?" a young man asked, reaching for the phone slowly. He couldn't tell if it was a sick joke or not, but it was too late for me to answer. I was already to the hall. Caleb was in pursuit in his socks. We made it to the street before we both stopped. Before it sank in that we had an audience.

I could tell Caleb wasn't going to hurt me now. He looked around him, shoulders slumped. "It's over now," he said.

I panicked. "I can fix this," I said. "I can fix this." We went back in the building, into the basement this time, through separate doors. I cried "I'll fix this," and headed upstairs.

I spoke to the resident assistants, shoulders shaking, and started sobbing. "I'm sorry," I said. "He's taking medication for his moods, and he's having problems. Side effects." This was true. "Please don't tell anyone. I know I don't have the right to ask you that, but please don't tell anyone."

One of the young women hugged me, so sweetly. "Of course," she said.

The young man looked at our apartment. "Is Reed in there?" he asked.

I panicked. "Yes," I said.

"Do you want me to go and sit with him?" he asked.

"Yes, please," I said.

I let him into the apartment and went downstairs to find Caleb. He was standing by the vending machines. He looked so tiny, so vulnerable. I couldn't believe what I had done to him. I had ruined his life. He would surely lose his job now.

"I fixed it," I said. I hugged him. He started sobbing and laid his head on my shoulder. The cloth of my shirt was soaked within seconds. He had never been vulnerable like that with me before. I held him tightly. "It's okay," I said. "I fixed it. Let's just go back upstairs."

I took him upstairs, then went to Reed's room. The resident assistant was sitting on his bed with him, playing Legos. Reed seemed oblivious. "We're okay," I said. "Thank you."

The resident assistant stood close to me, not yet a man, no

longer a boy. He looked at Caleb, standing in the next room. "Do you need anything?" he asked.

Yes, I wanted to say. *I need you to stop him. I need you to tell him to quit hurting me. I need you to protect me. I'm so scared. I'm just so scared.*

But I didn't say that. "I'm fine," I said.

He left, shooting Caleb a glance as he walked by, but Caleb wouldn't look at him.

Once he was gone, I broke down crying. Caleb was still so angry, I could tell. We had guests coming, and I knew I needed to clean myself up, put some ice cubes on my red and puffy eyes, cover my under-eye circles with concealer, change my damp shirt, practice smiling. My seven-year-old birthday boy was so excited.

Reed played quietly on his bed. It was what he always did during these rages. He stayed there as long as was needed. I went into the hallway, and Reed followed me. He moved in front of me, and I looked down at him. He reached out hesitantly, put his hands on my stomach, and looked into my eyes searchingly in a way he never had before. He was growing up, and his eyes disclosed to me that he knew. He knew what was happening.

"Mom?" he asked, still holding me gently, eyes still attached to mine.

"It's okay, sweetie," I said, reaching down to smooth his thick hair over his forehead. "I'm okay."

"I don't like it when the dogs climb into bed with me because they're scared," he said.

He looked so much like I had when I was a child, the same strawberry hair and big blue eyes. I thought of myself as a little girl in Idaho, a sensitive little girl who witnessed the sadness of the adults around her but who never imagined that her own future would contain so much heartbreak. In that moment, I knew. I knew we had to leave.

1

Blue

WHEN I WAS a little girl, my brother, Glen, had night terrors and sleepwalked; he also had chronic migraines. My mother spent her nights focused on his moon face, eyes creased with worry, dabbing cold rags on his head, guiding him back to bed, holding his shaking shoulders.

I had my night terrors, too, but they were silent. I woke in the middle of the night while the ghosts, the fear of everything that was out of my control, pressed down into my chest. I heaved and shook, but couldn't scream. I could feel them right above me; I could see them floating in corners. They never went away, even when I awoke.

Once Glen bolted down the hallway, screaming, and I watched from my doorway as my mother grabbed his hand and guided him back to his room. She couldn't wake him when he was like that. He looked at me—eyes wide open, the whites shot through with red—but dead asleep, he couldn't see me. I was invisible to them both.

One cold winter morning, I woke early and looked out the window above my bed into the darkness. The ice on the window cracked and splintered as I pressed my fingers into the frost, the tips leaving steamy imprints in tiny dots. I leaned in and made a shadowy ghost by forcing my cheeks into the glass and blowing through my lips. My ghost stared back at me as I pulled the blanket around my shoulders. I didn't want to get out of bed until the house had warmed, so I huddled under the covers and waited until my father had stoked the fire enough in the wood stove.

Every morning I listened for the sound of the radio and the fire crackling. School was only canceled if the temperature dropped to twenty below zero, and this would happen for days on end. When the deejay, "Leo the Lion," a middle-aged Mormon with a booming voice, announced that school was canceled again, I smiled to myself before jumping out of bed to play outside. The weather never stopped me; I wasn't afraid of anything but ghosts.

MY NEIGHBOR DANNY didn't like the cold, and this was a cold day. His aunt who he lived with was a lunch lady, and the family didn't have a wood stove. They couldn't keep their house very warm. My family was not rich, barely even middle-class, but my mother was a registered nurse, and my father worked for the US Forest Service, so compared to Danny's family, we had a lot.

For a while Danny couldn't come over anymore, because he had tried to touch what my parents referred to as my "private parts." Months earlier, Danny and I had been on the side of the yard where my parents kept their vegetable garden. We were hidden behind a row of tomato plants when he asked me to show him my "private parts." I didn't want to, but he told me that adults do it all the time. The older neighbor boys snickered in Danny's yard below, pointing at us. I had the feeling I was being tricked, but I was too young to know how, and I never turned down a dare, so I slowly raised my skirt, and then he dropped his pants.

His own "private parts" just hung there—pink and soft. I couldn't look away. He leaned his hips forward and said that we should rub our privates together. I stepped back quickly, because I *really* didn't want to do that. Just then my mother came rushing around the corner, her arms fluttering around her head like butterflies. She yanked my skirt down and told Danny, "Go home and never come over anymore." She hurried me inside the house, and then lectured me about how I should never let boys see my privates—no matter what. I nodded my head with a blank stare.

Trouble wasn't new to me. I was the difficult child. My brother, six years my senior, was the sweet and honest one. I never heard my mother yell at Glen like she yelled at me. I had a fury in me, always wanting things I couldn't have—a later bedtime, more friends, a different family. Once I chased my brother with an ice skate raised above my head. He locked himself in the bathroom, and I jammed the ice skate into the wooden door, sliding the blade down and leaving a gash that showed the lighter wood underneath. I was ashamed later, but I never let on that I was. I didn't want them to think I was sorry.

"She's got that redheaded temper," everybody said about me. My mother didn't like that, because she was a redhead too. "People make redheads like that," she said, "by the way they treat them." She may have been right, because she was just like me. She never backed down from a fight.

THE DAY BEFORE he tried to see my privates, Danny chased me around the house with a knife. He threw my doll in the mud, so I pushed him. Girl or not, I was ready to fight, but then he pulled a knife out of his pocket and said he was going to cut me. I could see in his eyes that he meant what he said. I ran as fast as I could, making three full laps around the house while screaming for Glen to help me. My brother was on the deck with his friends, and they were ignoring me as usual. I was pretty fast, could usually outrun any of the boys, but I was tiring, and Danny was gaining ground on me. I knew he was going to stab me. That he wasn't kidding. There was a cruelty in his eyes, and it wasn't like my anger, which burned in my chest but usually ended in tears and a trip to my bedroom. Danny's rage was something more.

Finally Glen stepped in, grabbed Danny by the shirt, and told him to leave me alone. Then Glen pushed me on my shoulder, hard, and called me a wimp. "He wasn't going to hurt you," he said.

I stood there with my shoulder stinging while this little knot in my stomach burned its way into the back of my throat. The burning was somewhere between anger and sadness. Glen didn't understand. He would always be bigger than me. He would always be stronger. I could be the toughest little girl on the planet, but I was still just a girl. I knew my mother wouldn't believe me, so I didn't tell her about Danny trying to stab me or Glen watching me squirm before he stepped in to help. I was afraid of Danny and his knife, but not enough to risk being called a liar. I might have been good at running away, but, even then, I wasn't good at asking for help.

AT THE SAME time, I knew I needed to be nice to Danny because his dad was dying. His own mother had abandoned them. Danny had lived with his dad in the house next to us, but when his dad got too sick, Danny moved in with his aunt down the street. Danny lived there with his brother, Wade, his sister, Bambi, his aunt, and his grandpa, who had Alzheimer's. He and his brother practically lived to come to our house to play basketball and eat all of my father's elk jerky.

Earlier that winter, we had come home from church and found Danny trying to cook a pizza he'd stolen out of the freezer in the garage over a fire in the backyard. His fire wasn't burning very well, though, and it just left a pool of melted snow. The pizza was half frozen, half soggy, and I thought that was the dumbest thing I'd ever seen anyone do. I thought my parents would be furious, but they weren't angry. They just brought him in the house and made him a ham sandwich. My parents cared about Danny in a way that I never fully understood. When they saw him, they only saw the vulnerable child. They didn't see the kid with the knife.

My mother called Danny's aunt, who sent his brother, Wade, over to get him. Wade was big, with stringy red hair, lots of freckles, and strong arms, and he scared me. His dog, Mimi, followed him everywhere, like a little white mop dragging around his feet. Mimi made Wade seem less scary, because he loved her so much.

ON THAT SNOW day, I put on my powder-blue snowsuit and begged my mother to let me go sledding. She said yes, but to come home by lunch. Outside, the air was so cold that the inside of my nose cracked and tickled. Glen was still sleeping. He could sleep all day.

I grabbed my sled from the garage and dragged it around to the front of the house. The snow looked so flat and soft and white, I couldn't resist. I stretched out my arms and looked up at the clear blue sky, palms facing upward, then let myself fall back, slowly at first, then faster. The sky stretched out endlessly above me, the world spinning. When I landed, the snow was hard. It was too cold and had crystallized into frozen shards of glass. Still, I thrust my arms and legs back and forth, dragging out an angel in the ice.

I wanted to be an angel, but I didn't think I was holy. In Sunday school, I had learned about possession. Possession happened when you didn't fill your body with the Holy Spirit. There was a scripture that read, "When the unclean spirit is gone out of a man, he walketh through dry places, seeking rest; and finding none, he saith, I will return unto my house whence I came out."

My body wasn't a safe house. I had awful thoughts all the time. I was jealous of my brother, and I knew jealousy was a sin. Sometimes, I wished that I had been given up for adoption by accident, and that my original family was frantically looking for me. When they found me, they would be so grateful and full of love that I would be the most special person in the world, and they would never know about my meanness and lies—how I screamed at my mom or blamed things on my brother. I knew it was a sin not to honor my mother and father, and that was what I thought was my worst sin.

At night, I worried that I had left a door open for the devil in my body. Before I fell asleep, I prayed for God to protect me, from the ghosts, from my nightmares, from possession. When I woke up with that familiar heaviness on my chest, I prayed again: *God, protect me. Make it go away.*

Yes, I was no angel. When I looked into the cold sky, I only saw one thin cloud stretching across it in lines. That cloud wasn't fluffy enough to be heaven, I thought. God would fall through a cloud like that.

A shadow appeared in my vision. It was Danny. He held out his hand and helped me up, but when I reached down for my sled, he started kicking my angel viciously with his sneakers until my angel was a mess of streaky footprints.

"Hey!" I yelled, ready to push him over into the snow, but I stopped when I saw his tear-streaked face.

"You've got to help," he said, gulping in air. "I let Mimi out, and she didn't come back. Now Wade's really mad at me. I looked everywhere, but I can't find her, and Wade says he's going to kick my ass. You've got to help me find her."

"I don't know," I said, looking up and wiping my arm across my nose, which was starting to run. "I was going sledding."

His eyes welled up with tears again.

"Well . . . okay," I said.

I brushed the snow off my legs. Danny was hopping back and forth from one foot to the other, so I started walking.

Danny pulled on me, and we hurried down the road. "Let's check my dad's house," he said. "Maybe Mimi went there."

Danny and I reached his dad's yard and picked our way through the snowy knapweed. At the door, I hesitated as Danny turned the knob. I had never seen a dying man before.

Danny opened the door, and light spilled from the outside into a dusty living room.

"You have to be quiet in here," he said. We stepped inside. The floors were linoleum, even in the living room, and there was a green vinyl couch, but no other furniture besides that. There were no curtains on the windows, but the room was still dark because the windows were dirty. From down the hallway came a deep, alien sound—a mechanical breathing that pulsed in and out—and Danny crept toward the sound. I followed him with my breath held, and he pushed open a door.

Inside the room, there was a chair that looked like a barber's chair, and Danny's dad was lying flat in it, while a plastic bubble-like shape floated near his head. The bubble was hooked to a machine that was making the breathing sound, and the bubble pulsed in time with the machine. The plastic expanded and rippled as though it would break, then contracted back into itself with a sucking sound.

Danny's dad was facing the window, but he couldn't see us. We inched closer, and I let my breath out in one big whoosh. He was smoking a cigarette, but through a tracheotomy. At the sound of my breathing, he looked over and took the cigarette out of his neck. He ignored me and pressed his finger to the hole. His voice sounded as though he had been sucking the helium out of a balloon. "What are you doing here?" he asked Danny.

"Mimi ran away, and we can't find her. I thought she might be here," Danny said. He was hopping from toe to toe like he had to go to the bathroom. I stepped back and pretended that I was invisible.

Danny's dad didn't look mad, but he looked tired. "She's not here," he said. "I haven't seen her. Isn't she with Wade at your aunt's?"

Danny looked down at his feet, ashamed. "I let her out," he said, "and I forgot to let her back in. Wade's checking the woods for her."

His dad's face got even paler then, and he quickly put his finger back in his neck. "You know how much Wade loves that dog," he said.

Danny's face went white, then pink, then white again. He shuffled his feet and took his arms out of his pockets, then put them back in quickly, rustling the nylon on his thin coat. He looked at his dad.

His dad turned his face away. "Just go home and help your aunt with Grandpa," he said. "Wade can find Mimi."

"Okay," Danny said, then turned to leave. He didn't hug his dad or say, "I love you." I knew Danny didn't see his dad much, and soon afterward, he died.

In the spring, my father found Mimi. She had frozen in the snow in a field just behind our house, and remained buried there until the snow thawed out. My father scooped up her little white body and carried her inside. When Wade arrived, my father placed Mimi in his arms like a baby. Wade didn't look so tough anymore.

Danny was standing behind him, crying. He was still the boy with the knife, but he was also the boy who was suffering, and I felt a softening toward him. I wanted to take away his anger, and his grief, and replace it all with love. I wanted to give him the hugs he had never been given. I wanted to be like my parents, who only saw his innocence. Maybe, most of all, I wanted him to forgive me because I couldn't save him.

ON THE NIGHT I met Caleb, I was twenty-six—no longer a girl—but I still carried the memory of Danny in my bones. The feeling of shame from when he exposed himself to me, the terror of knowing that he had come so close to me with that blade. And still, I wanted to forget his violence and love him through my fear. I wanted my compassion to be enough to spare him any more pain. I was a woman full of wants who wanted to love someone in a way that would heal us both.

THAT NIGHT, I sat in a booth by myself at the Neurolux in Boise, where I was attending college. I was sinking into sparkling red plastic that was easy to get lost in. My friend Kelly M. was dancing with a man. A flashing neon crown blinked above the stage behind them, the yellow glow of the lights hazy in the smoke. The darkness, the sweaty bodies, the slick plastic under my thighs; I wanted something to happen.

I stared greedily at the man. He wasn't handsome, but there was something about him. In a baseball cap and flannel shirt, he was different from the other men in this hipster bar. He looked more like the men from my hometown, men who could fell trees and chop cords of firewood, leaving thick layers of sawdust in the air and the sweet smell of fresh timber.

Kelly M. sidled up to him, swaying her hips. She had always been more confident than me. She reached out her hands and placed her fingers in his belt loops. Then, with a flourish, she pulled down his pants and danced off. Unruffled, he continued dancing alone in his boxer shorts, pants bunched up around his ankles.

I laughed, and Kelly M. danced over and slid into the booth next to me. "Who is that?" I asked.

"That's Caleb," she said. "You would love him. He's a fiction writer who lives in the woods in a little cabin he built by himself. He's exactly your type."

She waved Caleb over and introduced him to me.

We stayed until the bar closed, and then he walked me to my apartment. I invited him inside. On my couch, I sat close to him. He took off his hat. Only twenty-four, and he was already bald. He shyly ran his hand over his smooth scalp, visibly embarrassed. I reached over and glided my hand gently over his head, then smiled at him to show him that I didn't care. He leaned over and kissed me quickly, as though I would change my mind.

I didn't change my mind.

LATER, WHEN CALEB and I slept in his cabin in Idaho City, a former gold-rush town outside Boise, we could only spoon. His bed was on a wooden pallet just above the wood stove, but the heat radiating off the stove made our bodies too hot to touch. We only ever wanted to be touching, so we slept on the couch instead. He smoothed my thick hair down before laying his cheek against my head. He wrapped his arms around my shoulders. I had never slept so soundly.

"You fit me perfectly," he said. "It's like your body was made for mine."

We had only been dating for two months, and our relationship was still uncertain. Caleb would disappear for days at a time without contacting me. I knew that he didn't have phone service at his cabin, but I also knew that he drove into Boise three days a week for his MFA classes at the university. When he was in Boise, I could see his truck parked on the street, always under the same tree, but I didn't tell him that I knew he was in town. I didn't want to appear too eager.

Sometimes he would call me late at night after he'd been out drinking with his friends. He would want me to join him, or to come over to my apartment. Sometimes I would join him. Sometimes I would let him come over. Sometimes I would let the phone ring.

But when we were together, he was so sweet. He held me tight. He opened the car door for me. He called me honey. His West Virginia drawl made him seem gentlemanly. When his mother called while we were together, he always told her that he loved her before ending the call. This was so unlike my family. Love was something we kept compressed deep inside. Now I wanted to let Caleb into that darkness inside me.

IN HIS COZY cabin, I lay on the couch, covered in a blanket. Icicles, almost fluorescent in the moonlight, hung outside the window. Caleb played his guitar and sang "Pale Blue Eyes" by the Velvet Underground to me. My eyes were pale blue, and so were his. My eyes drifted shut, and I floated into that blue warmth. I was still not a good sleeper, still suffered from the night terrors of my childhood, often woke haunted by ghosts, real or imagined, hovering on the edge of my wakefulness, but in Caleb's cabin I slept soundly.

Later that night I woke to pee, but Caleb didn't have indoor plumbing, so I moved his arm from my shoulders, slipped on my boots, and let myself outside. I didn't feel like walking up the hill to the outhouse, so I squatted in the snow. The moon turned the snow into glitter around me while my gentle lover slumbered inside. Euphoria cracked in my chest. Such warmth. I raised my face to that moon and closed my eyes. Even then, the blue moonlight filtered through my eyelids.

This is a moment I will never allow myself to forget, I thought. When things get dark, I will always come back to this. I will return to this light.

I went back inside the cabin and curled my body up in the space that Caleb's body had left for mine. I don't know what I dreamed about. Not Danny. Not my parents. Not sadness. Maybe not anything.

2

Queen of Swords

SHORTLY BEFORE I met Caleb, I had my tarot cards read by a beautiful brunette named Shannon. Shannon also did Reiki massage, and when I was twenty-five and trying to heal from a painful breakup, she had given me one. By then I had stopped believing in the God of my childhood, but I still searched for answers outside myself. In many ways I was a skeptic, but Reiki and tarot appealed to that little girl inside me who still believed in God, ghosts, angels, and the devil.

During the massage, Shannon held her hands above my stomach, and her fingers quivered. She put me through a visualization exercise and told me to picture myself in a tower, to think of everything that caused me pain. She told me to visualize those painful memories as rocks, and to throw the rocks out of the tower, where they would land on the ground, be absorbed by the dirt, and bloom into flowers. In my imagination, I threw many rocks. There was much pain, but also many flowers.

She instructed me to visualize turning around and looking at the center of the tower, where a little girl sat. She said, "That little girl is you as a child. Go to her. Hug her. Treat that child version of yourself with the kindness that you would have for any child. Hug her like a loving mother would hug her and picture the walls of the tower collapsing."

It seemed to work. As I visualized hugging my child self, I thought of my mother. My shoulders shook with pain. My mother was an orphan: her father dead when she was seven, her mother dead when my mom was eleven. There was a part of her that she kept off-limits to me. It was as if the child of an orphan was an orphan.

A YEAR AFTER my Reiki massage, Shannon read my tarot cards. I was still single at that time, but had been with a series of lovers who didn't work out. Shannon and I sat cross-legged on the carpet of my apartment while she spread her cards into a map of my past, present, and future. It felt as if each time I drew a card for myself, the card was the Queen of Swords.

The Queen of Swords reaches out for someone, but holds a sword in front of her. Is it for protection or is it a weapon? Her face is repentant. Sorrowful.

Shannon instructed me to be careful. "Every person you sleep with," she warned, "will leave an imprint on you, a little piece of their soul. You don't want to take on a black soul. You don't want that darkness in yourself."

She told me to envision cords tying me to the people who had hurt me and then cut the cords. She instructed me to act this out physically. I made my fingers in the shape of a pair of scissors. Then snip. It was that easy.

That night, in bed, I started cutting the cords, my fingers working furiously, but the hurtful lovers sprang up too fast.

THERE WAS THE wolf biologist, a graduate student with whitish blond hair and a Scandinavian last name. His house was warm, the wood stove always burning during the cold Idaho winter. He had a soft beard that he would nuzzle into my neck, *grrr*ing, making me ticklish and giggly. I thought I could have loved him, but he had another girlfriend—the one who really mattered—in Moscow, Idaho.

There was Greg, the sociologist, who was the first man to tell me he loved me. When I told him about a man who had held me down when I was nineteen, Greg asked me if I wanted to use nipple clamps or other S&M devices. He assumed I wanted to be hurt again. As if being hurt was the thing I loved.

There was the fourth-grade teacher who liked to smoke pot before having sex. We spent entire afternoons in bed listening to Prince and touching each other. That relationship dissolved organically. It was only about sex, and I wanted more, but not with him.

There was the fish biologist, the only man I had dated who had consistent employment, a government job even, and he treated me kindly. At night I curved to his outline, wearing his stability like a blanket.

The security he offered me burrowed into my heart—crystallizing into love, or at least something like it. We had so little in common, but I would have spent my life with him. I wouldn't have been happy, but I would have been safe.

When he left, I bowed my head into my lap, curling into myself, digging my nails into my arms. *Not good enough*, the voice in my head said. *I was never good enough.*

Snip, snip, snip. There were too many cords for me to sever. I was so tired. I couldn't keep up with them; I fell asleep tangled in cords.

WHEN MY TAROT reading was over, Shannon put me through another visualization. She instructed me to think of the four elements—earth, fire, air, and water—and identify which element the men I had loved had in common. I closed my eyes, but all I could see was the ice of the rushing Salmon River in winter. I was the water trapped under the floes.

When I met Caleb, there was no ice in the way he held me, in the way he nuzzled his head into my hair. He was only warmth.

I had sex with Caleb too soon. I didn't know how to say no, and truthfully, I wanted to be with him, but still I lived with so much shame.

I remember being thirteen, riding in the back seat on the way to Wednesday-night Advent services at church. It was the middle of a cold winter, the night sky already black in late afternoon. Our headlights carved hollow tunnels through the drifting snow. Salt-N-Pepa sang on the radio about sex. About talking about sex. I bopped along in the back seat while my mom talked to my dad about work, but when I started to sing along, she swiveled around to look at me.

Her eyes glowed in the dark car. "This song is terrible," she said. "Just terrible. I can't believe it's on the radio."

I protested. "They are just saying we should talk about

sex—even the bad things. They're not saying we should have it."

"Well, there's no need to talk that way. How inappropriate. How sinful," she said, turning the dial off just as my favorite verse was starting, a verse in which a woman—any woman—uses her hot body for attention, or power, or love, or anything else she might lack. I didn't have a hot body; I was pretty average, in fact, but I liked the idea of it. Even at thirteen, I could tell the verse was a thinly veiled criticism of *that* woman, but I didn't care. I still wanted to be her.

But of course I never told my mom any of this. We never talked about sex—my mom and me—not that night or any night. Seven years later, a man—an acquaintance—put one hand over my mouth and the other between my legs. I gnashed my teeth, trying to bite, but my gnashing never pierced any flesh but my own.

That man didn't finish what he started. A neighbor overheard my screams and banged on the door, but I didn't blame the man. I blamed myself. I blamed myself for drinking too much. I blamed myself for sharing a cab with him. I blamed myself for letting him into my home. And because I blamed myself, I didn't tell anyone.

SHAME WASN'T NEW to me, and neither were secrets. I had been keeping them for a while. I was nearly abducted when I was sixteen, but I never told my mother. I couldn't stand to tell her something so horrible and not be believed, so instead I said nothing. I started carrying my stories beneath my rib cage in a physical manifestation that was somewhat like grief—a constant fluttering hummingbird's heart.

Around the time when I was almost abducted, Salmon with its one stoplight and dusty roads seemed like the quietest town in the universe. That May, we had just found out that a Subway sandwich shop was moving in, our first chain restaurant ever. While my father lamented the end of Salmon as we knew it, I was excited at the prospect of new life. Salmon was perched on the edge of a river in a wide, deep valley surrounded by mountains, and the only roads extending through town were small two-lane highways that wound over steep mountain passes in the high mountain desert and were punctuated by ghost towns with names like Leadore (which Caleb charmingly interpreted as "L'adore") and Gilmore—always some type of ore, a remnant from the promise of gold.

Salmon was so isolated that we lived under the shadow of a nuclear power plant, one of the few places in the country that created its own nuclear waste. When I was in the fourth grade, the town's water source tested positive for giardia. This was before the whole bottled water trend, so the local Budweiser distributer donated water in beer bottles for the schools. At home, we were told to boil our water for twenty minutes, but when I was thirsty at school, I would pop the top off a Bud and swig cold water from the brown bottle; it was the best water I had ever tasted.

At the same time, my parents made a joke about the nuclear power plant leaking and getting into our water supply.

They said we would glow in the dark. I didn't understand the difference between nuclear waste and giardia. At night I lay in bed, waving my hands in front of my face, looking for a hint of light coming from my fingertips, but there was nothing, and I fell into a deep sleep where, for a time, all of the ghosts that haunted my dreams were radioactive. I didn't tell my mother about the ghosts, and I never told her about the truck.

If I could have told her the full story, I would have said this:

I was thirsty because I had been riding my bike for an hour in warm silence. I was pedaling on a wide paved street flanked by lilac bushes and green striped lawns. It was dusk, and my bike made lazy arcs across the pavement as I rocked from side to side. I had friends who lived on that street, and I wanted to stop for a glass of water. I saw my brother's car parked in front of his friend's mom's house. Both boys were home from college. I looked into the windows from the street to see if my brother and his friend were inside, but the house was dark.

As I neared another friend's house, I heard a pickup truck driving behind me. It had the kind of loud gunshot engine that so many trucks in Idaho have. I moved to the side of the road so it could drive past me, but I heard the engine gunning with a revving sound. Instead of slowing down and moving away, the truck was speeding up and swerving toward me. I pedaled as fast as I could up a grassy hill into the yard of the town mayor's house. My bike slid in the grass, and

I tumbled off. The truck veered off and drove away. When I stood up, I looked down, and the truck had left deep grooves in the lawn.

I was shaken, but I figured the truck was probably being driven by a big dumb redneck who was trying to scare me. This was small-town Idaho in the 1990s, and the culture was still firmly entrenched in big trucks, chewing tobacco, and beautiful women.

I WAS NOT a beautiful girl. Or so I thought. That was why the rednecks didn't like me. That was why I got teased so much at school. That was why I wore my dad's big flannel plaid shirts. The bigger the shirt, the better it seemed at hiding my soft belly and large breasts. I was the girl who got breasts at eleven and endured countless bra-snapping humiliations. I was the girl who got ogled by grown men at my church confirmation when I was twelve. I was the girl who the men said looked so *womanly* now.

I GOT ON my bike and rode back into the street. The truck was gone, so I kept riding toward my friend's house. It was dark by then, and a dry breeze was ruffling my hair. I looked around me and realized that I was surrounded by homes with no lights on. As I neared the turn to Jackie's cul-de-sac, I rode underneath a streetlamp. At that moment, I saw him. He was sitting in his truck facing me with the headlights off, but the brake lights were glowing. At the same moment that I saw him, he saw me, and he gunned for me.

I heard the sound of his truck engine revving, and he was driving straight at me. Fortunately, I was right outside another classmate's house. I threw my bike down into the yard and ran to the door. As I banged on the door, the truck sped by. I didn't know what to do. I didn't want to get back on my bike, but there was no one home. Running to my friend Jackie's house wasn't an option. I could see the lights off there, too, and a football-field-size empty lot lay between the two houses. I crawled underneath my classmate's porch.

I had been afraid of small, dark spaces ever since I attended an Assembly of God day-care center. They had a big stage in the corner of the gymnasium. We were allowed to play anywhere in the gymnasium but not on the stage. One day, my best friend, Megan, dared me to run over to the stage. I was yanked back by a woman with frizzy hair who smelled of licorice and cigarette smoke. She looked in my eyes and said, "Don't play over there. The devil lives under that stage." I imagined the devil crouching, hidden in the dusty darkness below the stage—just waiting to get his hands on me. After that, when I played on my parents' large brass bed, I would stretch my legs out and jump off, all the while praying that the devil's skinny arms wouldn't snake out from under the dust ruffle to snatch at my legs.

Home wasn't a place that always felt safe. I was scared of the devil, and of ghosts, but mostly I was scared of my mother.

MY MOTHER WAS a good mother. She made us homemade family dinners every night—pot roast, or tater-tot casserole, or chili. I set the table, and we passed the meals clockwise—a constant exchange of energy and love.

She was one of the only non-Mormon mothers in town, and there was a lot of pressure on her to be like one of them— thin, wealthy, and focused on her children. The Mormon mothers sewed clothes for their children, and when I wanted one of the home-sewn rainbow-colored boatneck shirts that the Mormon daughters had, my mother took a sewing class so that she could make me one. It fell apart shortly after I started wearing it.

The Mormon girls went to church every Sunday, and so did we, but we went to the Lutheran church.

The Mormon girls had tight French braids, but when I asked my mother to braid my hair, she didn't know how to. She pulled too tightly, then too loosely. She wasn't gentle. She hurt me. No one teaches an orphan how to braid.

UNLIKE THE MORMON mothers, my mother worked. She worked long, hard twelve-hour night shifts at the hospital, and on those days her mood changed.

On day one of her three consecutive shifts, she was too tired to do much when she got home. My dad would buy burgers or fried chicken for dinner, or maybe he would make a meat loaf, which was one of the few meals that he knew how to prepare.

My mother would snap at me to clear my stuff out of the living room.

On day two, she would have more energy—would prepare a meal, would tidy the house, and would yell at all of us that she was tired of being "the only one who does anything around here."

On day three, she would come home and rage. "The house is a wreck," she would say. "What have you all been doing while I've been working?"

The truth was probably nothing. My father was laid-back, almost absent. He didn't make Glen and me do stuff around the house.

Sometimes my mother would scream at him, *I cannot do this on my own.*

Mostly, she screamed at me.

ON DAY FOUR, after her shifts had ended, I would wake to the sound of the vacuum. I could hear her rage in the rumble. I knew what was coming. She was going to scream at me, and if I talked back—which I usually did, because I was an angry child—she would slap me, or push me, or grab my arms and shake me.

I lay in bed as the sun grew unbearably hot, listening to the sound of the vacuum and not wanting to leave my room. The vacuum banged up against my door.

Bang.

Bang.

Bang.

It was time for me to get up.

BUT ON THE night of the truck, I was not scared of my mother, or ghosts, or the devil. I was scared of a different kind of devil as I crawled under the porch, pushing aside wet suits and kayaks, inhaling the smell of dirt and sweat. The earth was damp beneath my bare knees, and I could hear my heartbeat pounding in that dark space. I forced thoughts of spiders out of my head. Tall grass was scratching my face, and I shakily pushed it aside as I watched the road. The truck drove by again, then made a U-turn and cruised by the other way. I could see it clearly then. It was an old green flatbed truck. The hood was a different color, a sort of mixture between gray and rust. Through a dusty window, I could see the outline of a man with a dog seated next to him. I couldn't make out the details of his face, but I could tell that he was smoking a cigarette. I didn't know him, but suddenly I knew who he was.

As I crouched in the dirt, watching the man drive back and forth, I knew he was waiting for me. My bike was still on the lawn, and he knew I was somewhere nearby. A warning had been going around town. A couple of weeks earlier, some kids in my high school had shown up to class visibly shaken. They told me a story, too implausible to be true. They had been partying in the national forest. They were all high on acid, and having a great time, when a woman stumbled into their camp clutching a bloody T-shirt to her chest. She told them she had been kidnapped by a man in a flatbed truck with a dog. He blindfolded her and threw her in the cab, so she never saw his face, but she saw the truck, and she felt the dog with his hot snout pressed up to her neck.

The man took her to the woods and raped her before he bit off her nipple and left her there. Over the next two weeks, he kidnapped three more women. He kidnapped them all at night. Two of the women were in an alleyway behind a local bar. Another woman was in an alleyway behind a bank. In such a small town, the roads were dark at night, but they rarely felt unsafe. Still, this month, everyone was scared. The women all reported the same thing. They were blindfolded, taken to the woods, raped, and abandoned. The man had a flatbed truck and a dog. That was all they knew.

I huddled under that porch and watched the man drive by two or maybe three times. I was breathing fast and hard, and the smell of wounded animal pressed in on me. I scooted back farther. I knew he could see my bike in the yard, and I was pretty sure that he could see the house was dark. He knew I was hiding somewhere. He drove off, and I waited— time stretching into excruciating increments of worry. I didn't think he was entirely gone, but I didn't feel safe under that porch. If he got out of the truck, he would be able to grab me there, and no one would know. I waited a minute or so longer, and then I ran to my bike. I got on my bike and ped- aled as fast as I could, but I didn't know where I was going. I eventually ended up back at my brother's friend's house, where my brother's car was still parked outside. I hid my bike behind the hydrangea bush and ran to the door.

Just as I was about to knock, the truck rounded the cor- ner. I dove behind another bush by the door. I watched him drive slowly by, and I knew he hadn't seen me. My bike was hidden, but it was imperfectly hidden. If he drove by again, he would be able to see the bike between the leaves of the hydrangea. I prayed that my brother would be able to save me as I knocked on the door to the house, but there was no answer. My shoulders slumped, and I sniffled a little bit. I slouched down behind that bush and waited. There was nowhere else for me to go.

Just then, a truck drove by, and I shook. It pulled off to the side of the house, but when I looked at it, I realized it was Megan and her boyfriend, whose parents lived next door. I could see them talking in the truck, and I ran over and banged on the window. Megan gasped at the appearance of my white face in the window. She rolled down her window, and I told her what had happened, stumbling over my words in my haste to get them out. I got in Megan's truck and told her the whole story, and we drove down the street so she could see the tire marks on the mayor's lawn. She looked horrified. We turned around and headed back, making sure the windows were up and locked; the headlights searched the darkness. After driving past my bike and going another block or two, we saw him. His truck was idling in an alleyway just off the street. The lights were dimmed, but we could see exhaust coming out of the pipe. "He was cruising for you—" Megan's voice broke.

We slowed the car to try to get a license plate number, but he saw us looking at him and pulled out of the alleyway to drive off. Megan was determined to get the number. She drove after him, and as he sped up, we sped up—locked in a chase. When we got closer, we saw that his license plate was smeared with mud. By then, the man had figured out what we were doing, and he drove off so fast that we couldn't keep up. He was driving nearly seventy-five miles per hour in a twenty-five zone. We finally turned around and headed back, but I didn't want to go home. Megan took me to her house, and together, when we told her mom what happened, she convinced me to call the sheriff's department. I told a dispatcher all of the details. She was very kind, saying I had been lucky, and that she thought he might be the man they were looking for. I sat on Megan's couch for what felt like hours and talked to her mom while she nodded attentively. Megan's mom was different from my mom; I always told Mary everything that I didn't feel I could tell my own mom. But still, she said, "You should go home and tell this to your mother." I resisted leaving, staying as long as I could before she insisted I go home.

ONE MORNING, IN high school, I was watching an interview on *The Today Show*. The interviewee said that motherless mothers sometimes grow angry with their own daughters when they reach the same age that the mother was when her own mother died. So when my mother said, "When you turned eleven, it was like you went into your bedroom and never came out," I remembered that she had been eleven when her mother died.

When I got home, I said nothing. I didn't know how to, and I didn't want to face her skepticism. It's likely that Mary eventually told my mom, but even then, my mom wouldn't have asked me about the terrifying truck incident. Silence and screaming were the only things my family did well.

THE TRUTH IS that I never told my mom the whole truth about anything. I only gave her fragments. Still, those fragments were enough to earn her trust. I could see in her eyes that she believed in me, and that felt fine—except for the mushroom cloud still hanging over my head. I never told her about the man in the truck, or the man who held me down only a few years later, and I never told her about the lovers, or my loss of faith in her God. I never told her about my feeling that I couldn't be the daughter she wanted, or that she couldn't be the mother that I wanted.

My father was out of town on business that night, so I went into my mother's room and asked if I could sleep with her. It was the first time I had asked for that since I had been a small child, but she slid over and lifted the covers. She made room for me in that warmth, and I fell asleep to her quiet breathing. I thought that she could keep me safe.

Later, when Caleb was the man who scared me, I didn't tell her either. Not the first time, nor the second, and maybe not even the third. By then, I knew she couldn't keep me safe.

3

The Perfect Family

THE DAY THE test came back with two blue stripes, I put on my jeans and The Flicks T-shirt—the one with Alfred Hitchcock on the back—and drove to work. The Flicks was an indie movie house, and I worked there with artsy types who had lines of poetry tattooed on their forearms, dyed hair, and Converse sneakers. We wanted to make art. Children were not a part of our collective plan.

That morning I strode through the kitchen—past the assistant manager who was making curried sweet potato soup over the large gas range—stood before the espresso machine, turned the machine on to make a latte, and stopped. I didn't know if I could drink coffee. Coffee might be poison now. I listened to the whirring of the espresso grinder, the machine grinding the beans into fragments, and peered at my reflection in the brushed steel. *I'm not ready*, I mouthed.

A COUPLE OF weeks earlier, while we were sitting on my couch talking, Caleb's face suddenly started to flush. He looked down and brushed his hand over his head, which I knew meant he was feeling nervous or insecure. He looked up quickly and blurted out, "Kelly, I want to marry you."

I sat stunned. It wasn't a proposal as much as a declaration. We had only been together for five months, and because Caleb lived in the woods, we had only seen each other a few times a week. Twice, he had panicked and disappeared for a week or longer. The first time, I wrote his absence off to jitters. The second time, I called and left a message on his cell phone: "If you are interested in a relationship with me, you will call me today, and you will continue to call me on a regular basis. If not, then this is goodbye." He called almost immediately, and then showed up at my apartment that evening, his face and posture apologetic. He wasn't willing to lose me, he said. He knew that now.

Our relationship hadn't been idyllic or blissful, but in the moment after he had declared he wanted to marry me, all I could remember were the blissful parts. I looked into his wide blue eyes and remembered lying on that beige couch while he played his guitar and sang "Pale Blue Eyes."

I knew it wasn't responsible. We barely knew each other. He wanted four kids. He wanted to move back home to West Virginia. These were not things I wanted. But I wanted him.

"Okay," I blurted back, "but I'm not having four kids. I don't even know if I want kids."

He leaned back. "What about two kids?"

I could handle that. It was all theoretical, after all. "Okay," I said. "Two kids."

ONLY TWO WEEKS after the proposal, the test came back with two blue stripes. I went to work in the morning but left crying an hour later. I curled up in my bed and wept the entire day. Caleb was out fishing with a friend, but he came as soon as he got my message. He crawled into bed with me, his eyes crushed and vulnerable.

"Let's have an abortion," I whispered, pulling my knees into my chest.

"Let's get married," he said, smoothing his hand over his head.

"I'm not ready," I said. "For any of this."

He looked at me for a long time and then said, "Kelly, I think that if you have an abortion, our relationship won't survive that. We'll have to break up. I don't want that to happen, do you?"

I didn't want to break up. I felt so connected to him.

"Okay," I said. "We'll keep the baby."

"And we can get married? I don't want my child to be raised without married parents."

I nodded, but felt no joy. Only fear.

I DIDN'T WANT to be a mother, but I had more experience with children than most. I had been the go-to babysitter in my hometown, but that experience had taught me more about the lives of adults than it had about the lives of children.

I was only eleven when I babysat for Michael's parents. Still a child myself, I had just recently decided to put my Barbies away—I was too old for such nonsense—but sometimes, when a friend came over, we would take them out, clandestinely, and play. My brother was in high school, and he would babysit me when my parents left the house, but I thought I was ready to be a babysitter myself. I begged my mom until she relented. She knew I would call her if I needed anything.

Michael's hair glowed white, and when his arms wrapped around my neck, I inhaled the smell of baby in that softness. I had been taking care of him for six hours straight—the longest I had ever watched a child. While he napped, I tried to turn on the TV, but there was no reception. The house was small—oldish—and although it was tidy, it had that smell of a house that hadn't been cleaned in a while. It was sparsely furnished, no magazines or books to entertain me. I picked up the phone to call a friend, but there was no dial tone either. They didn't even have a working phone.

I flopped down on the green shag carpet by the stereo and looked through their cassette tape selection. I didn't recognize any of the bands until I came across something magical: Jon Bon Jovi's *Blaze of Glory*. I put the tape in and fast-forwarded. I lay on that carpet, sun filtering through the window in dusty lines, playing the title song, rewinding it, and playing it again. In the music video, Jon Bon Jovi stood on the edge of a cliff in the desert while the camera swooped over him, red rocks against blue sky. His hair was long and wavy, thrilling.

On a whim, I decided to go outside and reenact the video. I went into the yard, leaving the door open. It was a hundred degrees, and the heat hit me in a blast. There was no grass in the yard, only a scrubby tree. I held my arms out, lifting my face in supplication, *Going down! In a blaze of glory!* The world spun around me deliciously; I was transported by my fantasy.

But suddenly Michael was crying. Screaming. Shrieking. It was the loudest, most terror-stricken screaming I had ever heard, but when I burst through the door, Michael stopped. He looked at me smiling, raising his chubby arms. I swept him up, feeling loved, feeling like a mother.

I gave him a cup of apple juice, then took him outside to play. He poked around in the dirt, but mostly he followed me around. I tried to find things to play with and spotted a stick on the other side of the tree. I went to grab it, disappearing behind the tree. He shrieked again. I popped back out from behind the tree, and he quit crying immediately, smiling at me beatifically. I picked him up, and he nuzzled his head into my shoulder. It was the sweetest feeling ever.

I put him back down, then went back to grab the stick. He shrieked again when I disappeared, but this time I lingered, enjoying the feeling of being missed. When I came back, I cuddled him again. I enacted the ritual one more time, disappearing behind the tree, hearing him cry, then coming out to his cheers and smiles, picking him up, and cuddling him in my arms. I had so wanted his hugs but felt sick about my meanness.

MICHAEL'S PARENTS CAME home sunburned, smelling of beer, but happy to have had the day off. They paid me well. The poorer the family, the better they usually paid. I pocketed the money and kissed Michael goodbye. I walked home, dragging my feet in the dirt, the sun pounding on my head.

I knew I was going to be a terrible mother.

GRACE WAS THE child who scared me the most, with her round face and dark, knotted hair. She was plump, but her mother was skinny. When her mother picked me up, she swept gas-station coffee cups off the seat of her car, and the skin was so loose on her arm that I could see the two bones coming together at the wrist. Her trembling fingers looked like piano keys.

"Do you mind if I smoke?" she asked. I shook my head no. She was already smoking. I looked back at the house and my mom peeking her head out the screen door. She waved as we drove off.

Grace's house was somewhat shack-like. There were milk jugs in the yard with stray kittens lapping at the rims like nipples. In the corner of the yard, a heap of rusted-out farm machinery sat next to a pile of gravel. A large spray-painted plywood For Sale sign was propped against the shed.

"What's for sale? I asked.

The mother shrugged. "Everything," she said.

The mother and father were going out on a date, the first in a long time. The mother's fingers kept trembling. Her shoulders jutted out of a black leather vest.

The father looked at my breasts.

I WAS THIRTEEN. The summer before, my mom had taken me to a department store in Spokane, where I was fitted for a bra. It was confirmed; I was already a very embarrassed C cup. For the first time, we bought my school clothes in the teen section of the store, but I looked longingly at the children's

section. I picked out ten different variations of turtleneck. I
learned to slump my shoulders forward to hide my breasts.

GRACE'S MOTHER YELLED, "James, come on out and meet
the babysitter!" A large boy came out of the back room. He
was almost my age. We stared at each other awkwardly. The
mother shrugged. "He'll probably just hang out in his room,"
she said. "He doesn't really need a babysitter, but he won't
watch his sister, because he's a little shit." She yelled the last
part, rolling her eyes toward his disappearing frame as he
skulked back into his bedroom.

Grace hid in the kitchen. The mother finally dragged her
out, placing her firmly in front of me. Grace was tall, with a
moon face and big eyes. She seemed overgrown somehow. I
knelt down in front of her, trying to make eye contact. "Hi
Grace," I said. She twirled her hair, avoiding my gaze.

When she spoke, her voice was little. It was a toddler's
voice in a seven-year-old frame. "Hi," she squeaked, looking
down. I looked down too. Her foot traced a circle on the linoleum where the plastic was cracked and warped.

Later, we knelt on the floor in her bedroom, playing with
her Barbies next to a pink plastic dollhouse. "You be the
mommy, and I'll be the daddy," she commanded.

"Okay," I said. "Don't I look pretty?" I said, prancing Barbie across the floor.

She grabbed the Barbie out of my hand. "Not like that,"
she commanded. "Like this. Here, you lay on the bed." She
threw the Barbie onto the bed. "Now I'm daddy."

Her voice took on the gruffness of a male. "I'm daddy, and I'm going to beat you up." She pressed her Ken doll down on Barbie, rocking his plastic arms back and forth like punches.

I leaned back on my heels, quiet, a tightness in my chest. "Is that what your dad does?" I asked.

She looked up uncertainly.

"Grace!" I heard a sharp voice from the doorway. Her brother James was leaning in the door frame. "She's just playing," he said. "She always does that."

I looked back down at Grace, who was humming now, brushing out Barbie's hair. When I looked back to the doorway, James was staring at me, arms crossed. Eyes like dark pools in the shadowed hallway.

GRACE'S PARENTS COULDN'T drive me home. They'd had too much to drink. I was relieved they admitted it. They called me a BB taxi. In my hometown of 3,000 people, we had no real taxi service, but an enterprising couple sometimes gave folks rides for cash. The mother called them, but they didn't want to get out of bed, so I called my dad.

He answered the phone, flustered and sleepy. Then the excruciating part began. I had to wait on the couch for him to arrive. Grace's father went into their bedroom and fell down on the bed, calling out to his wife to come join him, but she sat next to me and made small talk. I tried not to look for bruises.

When my father arrived, I ran outside. His car was so warm, his presence comforting. He looked at me kindly. Noticing my relief, he said, "Maybe we should rethink some of your babysitting jobs." My father was a gentle man. A quiet man. Maybe too quiet. There was always a distance within him that I could not quite negotiate. Still, I was never frightened of him.

WHEN CALEB AND I started dating, I thought that he had the same gentleness as my father, but there was no distance for me to traverse. I felt as though no one had ever let me get closer. We never had long silences. We never went long without laughing.

We were engaged, but we hadn't even met each other's parents. I had told my mother about the pregnancy on the phone. I confessed to her that I thought I should have an abortion. "Oh, honey," she said. "You're twenty-six. You're not a kid. You can raise a child."

I don't know what she thought about the engagement. She knew me well enough to know that she couldn't have changed my mind. Maybe she was relieved that we were getting married. She couldn't have wanted me to be a single mother. That wasn't the way I had been raised. She didn't criticize or offer feedback. She supported me in my decision, and as with all of my other major life concerns, I didn't speak to my father at all.

Caleb and I drove to Salmon for a long weekend, so that he could meet my parents. I had been nauseous, but was also having food cravings. My first craving was for Doritos, but then the craving had switched to pie. In the weeks earlier, we had driven to a produce stand in Horseshoe Bend, a city about an hour away that had legendary pies. I bought a raspberry pie to go and cradled it in my lap on our drive home while the mountains gave way to desert hills that gave way to the broad green Boise Valley.

In three weeks, I ate my way through three counties.

On our drive to Salmon, we were on a winding stretch of mountain road, no towns in sight. We stopped in Stanley, Idaho, which has a population of less than one hundred. Caleb darted into the gas station and came back carrying a bag.

"I bought you something," he said.

Doritos.

"This doesn't taste like pie," I said as I crunched a chip into my mouth. He laughed, leaned across the car, and planted a kiss on me.

"You and your pie," he said. He stared at me for a long time, smiling, before starting the car and taking off.

WHEN WE ARRIVED at my parents' house, I acted as though everything was normal. I introduced Caleb, and my parents were warm and polite. I showed them my engagement ring, held out my hand, tiny diamond sparkling. I had picked it out myself at an antique store. It cost $350. I was proud of my thriftiness. My parents had raised me to be frugal.

My mother smiled. "Pretty," she said.

But when I turned to my father, I saw something else. His face was completely frozen.

My father was a kind man. He worked for the US Forest Service as a forester during the 1980s, which was a tumultuous period for logging in the community. Even though our neighbors' homes had signs in their windows that read "This Home Supported by Timber Dollars," my father's job involved shutting down the timber dollars. Environmental groups and changing federal policies were stopping the clear-cutting that had been going on for years. That kind of logging was not sustainable, and my father saw himself as a protector of the forest that he loved so dearly.

The timber boom had to end, but people left nasty messages on our answering machine. He received threats. At school I was called a forest circus brat, but he told me to ignore what they said. I thought he was the bravest person I knew. A quiet activist.

I had never seen him scared until that moment when I held out my hand, a used engagement ring on my finger. He was the calmest, most stoic person I knew, not prone to any displays of emotion, whether joy, sadness, or anger. I had only ever thought of him as brave, but in that moment, I only saw his fear.

STILL, MY PARENTS were kind people, and Caleb was charming, humble, and easy to talk to. He had a lot in common with my father. They had both been in Future Farmers of America. They both liked the outdoors. They had both grown up in the country. And like me, Caleb had been raised in a family that was deeply Christian. By the time we finished the weekend, the look of terror in my father's eyes had been replaced with relief.

Before we got into the car to leave, we all hugged. It was awkward. Caleb came from an affectionate family of huggers, but mine didn't quite know what to do. Finally, we all just patted each other on opposite shoulders and said goodbye. As Caleb and I pulled out of the driveway, I felt confident that everything was going to be okay.

ON OUR DRIVE home, just before reaching Boise, we came upon the scene of an accident. Flares marked the road around us. A police officer diverted our car.

Then I saw something. My hands fluttered to my stomach involuntarily. "Is that . . ." I asked Caleb.

He reached over and put his hand over my eyes, his other hand clutching the steering wheel. "Don't look," he said. His voice wasn't quite a shout, more of a groan. "Please, honey, don't look."

It was too late. I had already looked. Bodies. An adult body, and a baby's body.

Later, when we arrived home, I would discover that they had been the victims of a car crash in a road-rage incident. A Boise State football player and a man who had been drinking were trying to outrace each other. This family had been pulling into the intersection, and one of the vehicles slammed into their car, killing mother, father, and baby. Their last name was Perfect.

As we drove the remaining distance, the sun setting behind

the Boise foothills, I held my hands on my belly. I thought of Caleb's hand over my eyes. His first impulse had been to protect me. I told the baby inside me that his father would always protect him. I told the baby inside me that I would always protect him.

Caleb and I were silent. A new darkness surrounded us.

4

Runaway

CALEB HAD BUILT his cabin on his friend Cory's property, as had another friend, Dan. The guys jokingly called the connected properties the Compound, and even though I didn't really like Cory or Dan, we spent a lot of time there.

One night, at the bar where we'd met, Cory and Caleb grabbed Kelly M. and me from our table. Together, we all sped down the highway to the Compound, our bodies crammed on top of each other in Caleb's truck, the heat causing the windows to fog against the cold February air. When we arrived, Cory's wife, Carrie, was asleep with the baby upstairs. Cory took Kelly M.'s hand, dipping and swirling her into a dance. When Cory left to go to the outdoor bathroom, I leaned in and reminded Kelly M. that Cory was married.

The next morning everyone was in the house, including Dan, his girlfriend, and Carrie. Caleb and Dan made us all breakfast, and because Caleb remembered that my stomach was sensitive to milk, he told Dan not to give me any gravy. "Aw, it must be true love," Dan teased him, but Caleb just laughed, then swooped down to give me a kiss before heading back to the kitchen to help Dan.

Carrie smiled at me, but she looked tired. "Caleb and

Cory aren't good for each other," she said. "If Caleb wasn't so sweet, I don't think I'd be able to handle him living here." I remembered Cory flirting with Kelly M. the night before, and felt sorry for Carrie that she didn't realize that Cory was the bad influence.

WHEN CALEB AND I decided to get married, I told Caleb that we needed to move into town. We rushed to find a house that we could afford with a baby. It was not going to be the kind of home that I had imagined having with a husband and child. It was not going to have a porch swing, a breakfast nook, or a loft office. Because I had taken time off from college and changed my major a few times, I was still an undergraduate, with about a year to go before graduating. I had always worked, but the jobs didn't pay much, and Caleb's graduate teaching assistant salary didn't pay much more. Still, we wanted something close to downtown, preferably old, with a yard, but still close to coffee shops and galleries. These goals were nearly impossible to reach on our budget.

First we examined a dirty abandoned apartment with someone else's positive pregnancy test still resting on the back of the toilet. Next we toured a large, clean apartment, but it had baseboard heaters, broad white walls, sliding glass doors, and a sterile feeling that I couldn't abide.

We next looked at a house just outside the downtown area. The walls were smoke-stained, and cobwebs hung off the ceiling fan; when Caleb and I looked at each other, palpable sadness hung in the air between us.

Soon, though, I found it: an apartment in a two-story brick house, with ivy creeping up the sides. It had large windows and built-in bookshelves. A glass pane was missing from one of the bookshelves, and the carpet was old and stained, but the rent was cheap for Boise, and the location couldn't have been better. The landlord even said that he would throw in a couch that had been abandoned by the previous tenant. The tenant had reupholstered the couch with bright cotton stripes, and I coveted the wide vintage cushions and artificial cheer. I convinced myself that this first-floor apartment was perfect, but secretly, I was scared. It was old and run-down. It was the kind of apartment that graduate students would enjoy because of the "character," but not the kind of place where I would feel comfortable having other parents visit for play dates, not the kind of place where I would feel comfortable being a parent myself.

Cory had promised to help us move, but he didn't show up on the day, so we did it ourselves. A different friend arrived, and together he and Caleb walked the small amount of furniture that I had—a bed, dresser, desk, and my old couch—from my studio apartment to our new home.

The friend then made us pasta puttanesca, and we sat on the old couch in the backyard. I had cleaned the studio apartment by myself while Caleb and his friend moved the furniture, and my muscles sank into the couch as though they were one with it. I was so hungry that I lapped up the salty capers, enjoying the late-spring temperatures, and Caleb and his friend made me laugh. I was starting to feel that things would be okay.

As the night was turning to darkness, Cory arrived. He was drunk. He helped himself to some pasta. He helped himself to a beer. When he was finished with his beer, he crumpled the can and threw it at my feet.

"Is that where that goes?" I asked.

He looked directly in my face, then said, "Isn't that your job?" He licked the tines of his fork and threw that at my feet too. I looked at Caleb, who appeared not to have noticed what Cory had done. Just then Cory stood up and said to Caleb and the other friend, "Let's go to the Neurolux."

Caleb looked at me, and I shrugged, but I was resentful. Caleb left with his friends, and there I was alone, my belly full with pasta, baby, and worry. I remembered another one of Caleb's friends saying to me, "How did Caleb get *you* to date *him*?" I remembered the times that Caleb had disappeared for days. I remembered how horribly he had treated me before he realized that he was in love with me.

The next day Caleb and I argued. He told me that he had chewed Cory out at the bar, but I wondered why he had left with him in the first place. I started to cry, and my tears enraged him. "Quit crying!" he screamed, then threw a shoe box at me.

I ran out the back door, then stopped just as I reached my car. Where would I go? I was trying so hard to convince my friends that I was making the right decision that I didn't want to give them any reasons to believe that I was wrong. I stared at the car door for a long time, wondering what to do. We were getting married in a matter of weeks, and although I told my friends that I knew what I was doing was right, a voice inside me said just the opposite.

Before we moved to the new apartment, Kelly M. had come over to visit. She sat next to me on my couch, her hands clenched together in her lap, and said, "I was talking to Caleb's professor in his MFA program, and he doesn't think that you should marry Caleb. He doesn't think that Caleb is who he pretends to be." She looked into my eyes, the late-evening sunlight filtering in through the blinds casting stripes across her face. I didn't want to hear this.

"I don't think that you should marry him," she said. "You can raise this baby on your own. I know that you can."

I knew that she was coming to me out of love, but by then I had worked so hard to convince myself that I was making the right decision that I couldn't even consider changing my mind.

Caleb was so sweet, so tender. No one had ever held me like him. No one had ever said the things that he said.

You are the most beautiful woman I know. You are so smart. You are so sweet. You are so much more to me than all of the other women I've been with. I wish that I had never been with anyone else, so that you could be the only woman I've ever touched. If I had known that you were in the world, I would have saved myself for you.

I would have laughed had a friend reported this kind of love talk, but when I stood next to Caleb, and he tucked my head underneath his and said, "Your head fits perfectly underneath mine. It's like our bodies were made to be together," I believed him.

To a woman who had been hurt so many times, love like that was utterly uncommon. His words were a balm; they made me feel safe. No one else had ever loved me like that. No else ever would again.

He also said, "All of the other women I've dated have been bitches," and I believed that too. I thought that meant I was special.

I LOOKED BACK at Kelly M. "I need you to support me," I told her. "I need you to have my back."

"Okay," she said, giving me a hug. "If that's what you need, then that's what I'll do. You know that I love you. I support you no matter what."

I TURNED AROUND and went back into the apartment, where Caleb took me into his arms and held me tightly.

"I was wrong," he said. "I won't do it again."

I believed him. I had no other choice.

A FEW DAYS later, after the phone service was turned on in our apartment, there was no dial tone. When the repairman from the phone company opened the box, he discovered the problem. The wires had been cut, and they hung loose like tattered veins.

Later that day, standing over the sink in the dimly lit bathroom, I pulled the chain hanging down above the mirror to turn on the light. Immediately, a current shot through my body, not painful but an uncomfortable zap. The light buzzed and flared. The pads of my thumb and forefinger were covered with tiny black, beaded burns, the smell of burned skin nauseating. I backed out of the bathroom with my hands over my belly, hoping that the baby was okay. I wondered if I should see a doctor, but my mother reassured me that I was probably fine.

When the landlord came to fix the wires, he shook his head, telling me there had been an "incident" with the last tenant, an immigrant from Holland who had "lost his mind a little." I didn't want to ask if this was code for suicide. Soon I noticed evidence everywhere of the man's illness. In the bathroom, the wallpaper had been torn down in fits, and in its place, wrapping paper was stapled helter-skelter to cover. I couldn't fathom how I had missed so many signs of his darkness. The kewpie-doll wrapping paper seemed to stare at me. The figures had wide eyes, shuttered eyelids, perfectly formed curls, and limbs that were bound to their plastic bodies with glue.

ONCE WE HAD fully moved in, I lay on the brightly striped couch that I had coveted when I toured the apartment. I had never committed to anything in my life, but now my belly blossomed outward, the most final of all commitments. I was miserable. I didn't wear pregnancy well. I was nauseous most of the time, taking long naps every afternoon, and although I had always been very active, I didn't want to exercise. Many of my friends had quit coming around. None of them had children, and they weren't interested in children or in people expecting children.

One of them told me that Caleb and I were "breeders."

LONELINESS TOOK ROOT. I saw the ivy climbing the brick exterior of the house and felt choked by it while my hands caressed my taut belly. We had our first sonogram, and the baby's heart beat so fast that I looked at the doctor in alarm. She laughed. "That's completely normal," she said, but that *thumpa-thump* made me realize that my body was now a home. I knew that I couldn't run away from what was taking place inside me, or from what was taking place outside me.

I'D ALREADY SPENT a lot of time running away. At four years old, I ran away from a babysitter while my parents were on a date. I crouched in an empty lot filled with sagebrush behind our house and watched as the babysitter drove by slowly, calling out my name through the car window. The second time, I was eight. I filled my red nylon backpack with toys and left. Running away turned out to be easy; I simply left the yard. And even though I kept looking behind, no one came chasing after me, so I continued walking. Sweat dripped down my spine underneath the pack, so I took it off and shifted it in my arms, eventually choosing to drag it by one strap. I had just turned a corner when Wade, Danny's older brother, came riding his bike after me. He skidded to a stop, spraying gravel onto my shoes.

"Your dad told me to tell you to come home," he said.

"Fine," I said, handing him my pack. "Will you carry this?"

When I arrived back at the house, my red backpack was waiting on the steps for me. My father had been kneeling at the garden, yanking carrots from the soil. He barely looked up, "Where were you?" he asked.

In the sixth grade, I ran away for real. My mother and I had been in a huge fight. "I hate you!" I screamed.

"You're ungrateful!" she screamed back. "When I was your age, I didn't even have a mom."

I shut up then, but didn't tell her what I was really thinking: *I wish that I didn't have a mom.*

This particular fight was on day three of her night shifts. When she got home, she asked me multiple times to take my laundry out of the dryer, but I was immersed in a book and ignored her. She burst into my room screaming that I never listened to her, grabbed my book, threw it away, and then dragged me to the dryer by my hair. I was scared of her when she was like that, but I never told her that. I told her I hated her instead.

Later that night, I had my friend Jamie leave a bag of food on her back porch, and then I snuck out my window at night, retrieved the food, and hiked into the mountains above our house. I couldn't tell how far I had walked in the dark. I hadn't carried a flashlight, but I could hear the creek gurgling beside me, so I had a basic idea of where I was headed.

I didn't have a plan, but the Idaho mountains were filled with abandoned homesteads and cabins, so I hoped to find one to stay in. Soon I grew tired and decided to sleep. I laid my sleeping bag out in the dirt and crawled into it, using my backpack as a pillow, the dark sky hanging above me, stars glittering through the clouds. By then I was scared of the darkness, but I was more scared of going back. I knew that I would be in trouble. Then, in the distance, I heard branches breaking, and I saw lights swirling in the darkness. Voices called out, and I recognized one; it was BJ, my parents' best friend from church and my English teacher. Her panicked voice cried out, "Kelly." She'd been a trained singer, and her voice echoed in chords. A chorus of voices arose. *Kelly. Kelly. Kelly.* The voices grew closer, but I didn't move or make a sound until the flashlights disappeared.

The next morning, I awoke to sunlight and a growling stomach. When I ripped open the bag, I found corn chips, three cans of soup, and no can opener. I knew I had to go home.

When I arrived on the stoop, my mom opened the door, face drawn and puffy. She didn't hug me or say anything. She just tossed some clothes at me. "You're going to school."

At school, the principal, a gentle old man, came up to me and put his hand on my shoulder. "I heard you gave everyone quite a scare there, kiddo," he said.

I scrunched my eyes, trying not to cry, furious at myself for my embarrassment.

"Hey," he said, giving my shoulder a squeeze. "You know we all love you, right?"

I looked back at him and nodded. "Sure," I said. "I know." But I was lying.

I RAN AWAY again after dropping out of college one semester in. I'm not sure exactly why. I had wanted to go to a small liberal arts college in Ohio, but my parents convinced me to go to the University of Montana, close to home. I spent my days sleeping in my dorm room, tormented by feelings of inadequacy. Shy and anxious, I didn't know how to take care of myself. I didn't turn in assignments, even when I had completed them, because I was convinced they would be imperfect, and I was resentful that I wasn't at the school I had wanted to attend.

I yearned for something bigger than the valley where I had been raised, and I wanted to redeem myself for my failed semester. I got a refund from the University of Montana, and I took that refund and decided to go to Europe with a friend. I didn't even tell my parents. Our relationship was nonexistent by then. They had to find out from someone else, but once they did, in spite of their anger, they drove me to the airport, and later, when I called my mother from a pay phone in Rome and told her that I was out of money, she said that they would wire me some. A motorcycle drove by, and as the driver catcalled me, I heard the panic in my mother's voice when she cried out from across the ocean, *Are you all right?*

AFTER I RETURNED from Europe, I went home and lived with my parents. We all pretended that nothing had happened, and soon a friend living in Portland, Oregon, convinced me to move there. I had a couple thousand dollars that I had saved up from summer jobs, and I had never lived for long in a real city and was intrigued.

When I told my parents about my move, they thought it was a terrible idea, but they were defeated. By then I was on a daily dose of antianxiety medication. The pills didn't change much for me, but the constant lurching and fluttering anxiety in my stomach that had kept me from eating or sleeping for days abated. I stopped lying in bed shaking at night and digging my fingernails into my forearms to calm the trembling, but I still found it hard to make decisions. I fought the impulse to run away, but I knew that I needed change, and running away was the only option I could think of.

IN PORTLAND, I found a job in a downtown department store, then answered a classified ad in the *Willamette Week*: "Roommate Wanted. Creative household in old Victorian. Northwest Portland, off 23rd. Only $300 a month, utilities included." Northwest Twenty-Third was the hippest street in Portland at the time, packed with ethnic restaurants, coffee shops, and vintage clothing stores. I called and asked for a time to take the tour. The raspy female voice on the other end of the line was decisive. Any time.

HER NAME WAS Liza, and she showed me around the house. She was in her late twenties, with reddish-pink dyed hair. She wore fishnet tights, black vinyl boots, and a black miniskirt that just barely covered her butt cheeks, along with a tiny tank top that she oozed out of. Her voice had the huskiness of a smoker, and the house reeked of menthol cigarettes, but she assured me there would be no smoking in my room. *My room.* I thrilled at the sound. Already mine.

Smoke and dust clung to the drapes and furniture, and the hardwood floors seemed to slope at inappropriate angles that straightened out suddenly when I blinked, as if they knew I was watching. The living room was shaded, but when Liza pulled back the heavy drapes, light tumbled through the beveled glass of a deep bay window and sprawled lazily across the floor. Rainy Portland can be a dark place, but this light delighted me.

Liza and I climbed the heavy wooden stairs, and I palmed the original mahogany banister until we reached the landing, then the bathroom. There was a claw-foot tub with no showerhead and an inky reddish-brown stain that darkened near the drain. When I looked at the toilet, menstrual blood floated in the water. Liza's eyes followed my gaze, and she flushed, apologizing.

"There's no shower right now," she said. "But I'm going to have the landlord put one in this weekend."

When Liza opened the door to my room, I saw a bright open window with the branches of a tree draped outside. There wasn't much of a view, but the leaves let in just enough light to illuminate the room.

"Can I paint it?" I asked.

Liza shrugged. "Sure, you can do whatever you want."

I smiled, "Great, I'll take it. Can I move in immediately?"

Liza's mouth gaped, surprised. "Really?" she said.

I SOON DISCOVERED that Liza and her boyfriend were trying to quit heroin. Liza's best friend had recently overdosed and died on the same stairs that I climbed every day. Chad fared a bit better than Liza. His construction job kept him busy, but Liza was home alone, and she was getting itchy.

She'd taken to drinking 40s of malt liquor, and they built up on the back porch, skyscrapers of bottles piled in front of the kitchen window. The dim Portland sun peeked through the varying shades of glass and refracted into the kitchen, leaving a prismatic rainbow on the dirty floor.

WHILE LIZA DRANK downstairs, I hid and read on the air mattress in my room upstairs. Once, two women were yelling at each other in the apartment across the driveway. I lifted my head and watched them argue through the open window. Loneliness gnawed at my chest; it was the grandest fight I had ever seen—screaming, throwing, and embracing. I felt so alone. I would have given anything to have someone to fight like that with. I couldn't look away. One of the women headed toward the door, and the other fell to her knees, sobbing.

"Don't leave me. Please don't leave me. Please."

The woman stopped at the door. She turned around and started to walk back toward her lover. When she got close to the window, she looked up suddenly, peering through the window. I was caught.

"What are you looking at?" she screamed into the space between us. "What the fuck are you looking at?"

SOON I STARTED visiting with Liza on the couch in the evenings, when I got home from work. The filthy couch was horrifying, but I sat down anyway, trying to inhabit as little space as possible. Liza was going out of her mind trying not to use, and my company comforted her. She was lonely and never left the house. But she had stories to tell. So I listened, while she talked and swigged 40s of malt liquor. Courtney Love had lived in the house. "Courtney was a real bitch," Liza said. "She treated us all like shit, then she left without paying her rent. She's only famous because of Kurt Cobain. There was nothing special about her at all."

I didn't know if the story was true, but it fascinated me nonetheless. Kurt Cobain had killed himself only three years earlier, and I had grieved like a sixteen-year-old—driving by myself at night, stopping to sit by the Salmon River on a sandy bank, watching the dark water rush by, and wondering why life seemed to hurt so much.

Light filtered over Liza's face as she told me her stories;

decay registered in wrinkles around her mouth and her eyes. She wasn't beautiful. Not even a little bit. But she was sad, and that seemed to count for something.

I WANTED TO help her. I *knew* I could. Once, on my day off, I invited her to accompany me to the department store where I worked. I needed to pick up my paycheck, and she hadn't left the house in days. To my surprise, she agreed, but she looked bad. Her hair was greasy, her clothes dirty and revealing. When she caught someone staring at her on the bus, she stared back confrontationally.

I didn't understand how she must have felt. I was unremarkable. No one had ever stared at me.

When we walked into Meier & Frank, with its high ceilings and polished brass, my coworkers stopped to say hello, looking curiously at Liza. We headed toward the elevator, but I could tell she was nervous.

"Are you all right?" I asked.

She giggled. "I'm not supposed to be here," she said. She twisted her hair. "I'm eighty-sixed from this place. I was caught shoplifting here."

I said nothing, but I quickened my stride, praying that we could get to the payroll office and get out of there before we were noticed.

When we got back to the house, Liza opened another 40. "I'd really like to lose some weight," she said.

"Do you want to get a membership at a gym with me?" I asked. "We could work out. It would be fun."

She smiled. "Let me talk to Chad," she said. "But that actually sounds like a good idea."

"Great," I said, a big grin stretching across my face. "This is going to be great!"

THE NEXT MORNING Chad handed Liza one hundred dollars. He was thrilled. On his way out the door, he stopped and smiled at me. "You're good for her," he said. And I finally felt good about myself. I felt noble.

Liza and I rode the bus to the gym. When we walked in, we got lost trying to find the membership desk. We wandered around the halls until an employee stopped us, "Can I help you?" she asked, staring pointedly at Liza.

For the first time, Liza didn't stare back. She shrank.

"Where's the membership desk?" I asked, trying to appear confident.

The woman pointed up the stairs, then walked away. I acted as if I hadn't noticed her demeanor, but Liza's face was crushed. The guy behind the membership desk looked surprised when I inquired about getting a membership. He stared at Liza, then at me. "We have strict membership policies," he said.

I didn't understand.

"No loitering," he said. "And you need to have an address."

It took me a moment to realize he thought Liza was homeless.

"We have an address," I said. "We're roommates."

Liza spoke up. "Look, I have the money."

He got uncomfortable. "Okay, fill out this paperwork. I'll need to see a piece of mail and your ID."

Liza glanced at me, ashamed. "I don't have an ID. I lost it."

The man behind the desk leaned forward. "You can't get a membership without an ID," he said.

"Why does that matter?" I asked.

He held up his hands in surrender. "I don't make the rules."

"Just forget it," Liza mumbled to me. "They obviously don't want me here, anyway."

He nodded at me. "Do you still want the membership?"

I shook my head. On the bus ride home, Liza's silence accused me of what I already believed. I had hurt her. Maybe I hadn't even been trying to help. Maybe I had just wanted to make myself feel good about helping this woman who seemed broken.

When we got to the house, I went to my room, grabbed a book, and left for a coffee shop. Liza didn't say anything when I walked out the door. I spent the rest of the afternoon drinking coffee, reading, and walking down NW Twenty-Third, looking in the store windows filled with sparkling chrome, chandeliers, and mannequins. I didn't want to, but when dusk fell, I returned to the house. I straightened my clothes, tried to put on a casual smile, and opened the door.

Liza was sitting on the couch. Her eyes were slits, her body limp. She slurred at me, "Heey."

I KNEW IMMEDIATELY what had happened. I went upstairs and locked the door. Soon I heard Chad come in. It was quiet for a while, but then the noise rumbled up the stairs, exploding into screams. "Where's the money? Where is the fucking money?"

I didn't hear Liza's reply, just a crash. I jumped up and ran down the stairs and out the door, my heartbeat pounding in my ears, until I reached a pay phone. I called my parents collect. I was sobbing. "Mom," I sobbed. "Mom."

Her voice was calm. She would pay for a local hotel and be there the next day. She said not to worry about the twelve-hour drive; she and my father would drive all night. Her voice wasn't angry or reproachful; she was relieved that I had asked for help.

When they arrived, my parents didn't hug me. They weren't huggers, and I had been holding that against them my entire life. Hating them for all those missed embraces, treating them as if they hadn't loved me enough. But here they were, packing my things into their car while Liza cried. We were quick, gone in less than an hour.

Liza screamed at me on the way out, "How are we going to pay our rent?" I started to turn. I didn't know what to say. My mother grabbed my arm. "Don't look back," she said. "Just don't look back."

My parents found me a clean studio apartment. They cosigned the lease, took me to a grocery store, and stocked my refrigerator, then took me out to dinner at a restaurant downtown. They acted as if nothing had happened, just the same as every other time I had run away, but even in the face of their generosity, I knew that I would continue to hold my mother's temper, and my father's reticence, against them. I didn't know yet how to forgive.

A few months later I moved home just as impulsively as I had left, and as always, they accepted me back without judgment. I went back to college after a while. This time I was serious. By then I had learned how to manage my anxiety. I got a 4.0, I worked in the writing center, and I had professors advocating for my future. I felt that I could do anything I wanted.

Then I met Caleb.

THAT SUMMER, CALEB and I tried to make our run-down apartment into a home. We wallpapered over the wrapping-papered walls in the bathroom. The landlord fixed the short circuit in the light above the sink. We hung art and cleaned the carpets.

It was a hot summer—with temperatures exceeding 110—and we didn't have air-conditioning. Caleb took a job painting houses and worked all day. I was only working part-time, and spent long afternoons napping on that rainbow-colored couch.

One morning I opened the door to let in some cool air before the afternoon heat arrived. A hummingbird flew in and buzzed around confusedly. It finally saw the big glass window in the corner of the living room and flew toward it. I watched the bird bang its head helplessly on the glass. It kept trying, but it didn't learn. I reached out and gently closed its quivering body in my hands, its wings pulsing against my fingers, as fast as the heartbeat that was living inside me. I could save this bird. I walked outside, opened my hands, and the hummingbird flew away. I rested my palms on my belly, then headed back to the couch for a nap.

I baked in the harsh sunlight that fell through the same big window, and sleep came in fits. I tossed, clothes sticking to my back, and dreamed of the ghost of a woman floating in the corner of the room, in a black dress with black hair. In my dream, she looked kind of like Liza, but she also looked like me. How could I possibly have saved Liza when I hadn't even been able to save myself?

When I woke—with the baby pressing down on my bladder—I stumbled to the bathroom in a nap daze. Once in there, I looked at the wallpaper that Caleb had so lovingly hung. I had chosen white wallpaper with ivory stripes, and the room looked brighter, cheerier, but even that wallpaper couldn't disguise the chaos underneath. If I looked close enough, I could still see bound-up girl-dolls staring back at me, trapped under those clean white stripes.

5

Would I Rather?

Would I rather?
A. Marry Caleb?
B. Become a single mother?

A. Get married in my parents' church, where the minister once gave a speech on how women should serve their husbands?
B. Be married in a field, with a ceremony performed by Caleb's loathsome friend Cory?

A. Inconvenience my mother-in-law, the teacher, by setting the wedding date on a weekend before the end of the school year?
B. Be visibly pregnant on my wedding day?

A. Admit to my friends and family that I'm pregnant?
B. Cry alone at night?

A. Agree with my mother between sobs that I don't have to go through with this?
B. Tell her that, yes, I do.

6

Saved

IN THE FALL the summer heat left the Boise Valley, and the evenings cooled while my belly continued to grow. Boise, the City of Trees, derives its name from the French *les bois*, "the woods." When settlers discovered the Boise Valley, they found, amid the dryness of the high-country desert, a river flanked on either side by trees, green and lush amid the crackling brown hills.

Fall was Caleb's favorite time of year. In West Virginia, his home state, the forests changed more dramatically than in Boise—yellow, orange, and gold ballooned over the hollowed-out hills, the blown-off mountaintops, and the pollutant-stained but beautiful rivers. But what Caleb loved more than the changing leaves of the forest was hunting season.

Caleb's parents owned one hundred acres in Appalachia, and with his father's help, Caleb had built a cabin on his family's property that was much like the cabin he had built in Idaho City. He and his father felled the trees themselves, sanded them, and then lovingly fit the pieces together. When Caleb and I married in May, his grandmother had given me a family photo album. In it was a photo of

Caleb's immediate family sitting on the front porch of the cabin, dressed up to look like settlers: Caleb and his father in white shirts and suspenders, his mother and sister in prairie-style dresses, and Caleb with a gun in his hands—either a muzzle-loader or a rifle, I can't remember which. Maybe it was his father who held the gun, or perhaps it was both of them. All I remember is that gun pointed upward, seemingly cocked. When I looked at that photo, I thought, I'll never fit into that family.

THE FIRST TIME I visited West Virginia with Caleb—in the hot, humid August after our wedding—the preacher at his family's Baptist church said to me, "So I hear that you're going to be a *working woman*," and I shrank from his disdain. The church was a simple white building, located in the hills just above Caleb's family farm. Caleb's family lived in a hollow, or, as the locals called it, "holler"—narrow, packed tight with greenery, and pulsing with birdsong, crickets, and the rhythmic echo of frogs.

The congregants at the church were friendly working-class people who treated me with kindness, but Caleb was beloved—one of the few residents of the holler to have ever left—and it was apparent that he was expected to move home. When I agreed to marry Caleb, I told him that I didn't want to leave the West, that the national forests and vast blue skies were a part of my identity. He agreed and reassured me that he, too, didn't want to leave. Still, it was evident at that church that they had other plans for him.

During the service, the preacher asked everyone in the congregation to close their eyes. He then instructed us to consider whether we were saved, and whether we had ever gone to the front of the church to offer testimony. I wasn't even sure what "testimony" meant. Lutherans were private; we only went to the front of the church for communion. Later, when I asked my mother what it meant to be saved, she said merely, "Don't listen to them. You were saved when you were baptized as a baby."

The preacher told everyone who had already offered testimony to keep their eyes closed and raise their hands. He then said, "If your hand isn't raised, then open your eyes." I opened my eyes, and he stood before me, in front of three simple wooden crosses. "If your eyes are open, then this is your chance to come to the front," he boomed, his eyes on me.

I looked around me. I was surrounded by people shaking, eyes pressed tightly closed, hands held up with urgency. Caleb sat next to me, eyes also open—hands in his lap—and I realized the preacher was staring at both of us. Caleb stared back, defiant, angry.

Finally, a man broke the silence and rushed to the pulpit, weeping. He fell to his knees, and the preacher put his hands on his shoulders, called him "brother." I shrank into my seat. Caleb reached over and squeezed my hand, then wound his fingers into mine.

WHEN FALL ARRIVED in Boise, only a couple of months after that day in church, I was in my third trimester of pregnancy. I didn't have the energy to do very much, but Caleb nurtured me so well. He grew to love cooking, especially slow cooking, and he would simmer meals on the stove all afternoon—soups like white bean stew, or roasted tomato— accompanied by crunchy baguettes and spinach salads. When we met, he had been a picky eater who lived off McDonald's and venison, but he had transformed his diet for me. If I had a yen for something, he made it for me. He was the most indulgent man I had ever met. He rubbed my tight shoulders, massaged my feet. At night he curled his body to mine, held his hand on my stomach. He leaned in and spoke to the baby when my skin stretched and moved outward in the shape of a tiny foot.

OUR LANDLORD SOLD our apartment out from underneath us, and we were forced to move, but that was a blessing. It gave me a reason to ask my parents for help. As they always had before, they helped us move into a smaller but cleaner apartment, and they generously supplemented our monthly income, so that we could afford the slightly higher rent. In the new place, with clean paint, wooden floors, and a room across the hall that was perfectly sized for a nursery, I no longer felt scared.

CALEB WANTED TO go hunting before the baby came. One Sunday afternoon, he asked me to ride with him while he drove into the mountains and scouted for elk. He put his muzzle-loader into the back of my Isuzu Trooper—just in case he saw anything—and we drove toward Idaho City, rain drizzling on the car, then turned off the highway onto a forest service road that wound deep into the mountains. As we drove deeper and deeper into the forest, I realized that we were nearing Atlanta, Idaho, where I'd been with another man, Greg, the sociologist who was the first man I had ever loved.

I WAS TWENTY-TWO years old, and he was thirty-three. Greg, who was working on his PhD dissertation, strongly believed the West could be saved by timber. *Trees Are the Answer!* was the title of a book he gave to my father. He was brilliant—the only person I'd ever met who earned a perfect score on his SAT but still listened to the Magnetic Fields and Stereolab— and I was mesmerized by his intelligence. Greg came from wealth, but was researching the few remaining Idaho saw- mills. Greg was a man torn between the world of privilege he was raised in and the working-class world he was researching. He was torn so passionately that it drove him to drink.

GREG AND I needed to set up camp, but first we decided to stop at the local bar. We walked up to the screen door, and a large dreamcatcher covered in some kind of white fur— coyote, maybe—blew in the wind. I pushed through the door, and the din of conversation stopped. Everyone was looking at us. I looked around. The cabin seemed to be one part tavern, one part café, and one part grocery/knickknack store.

Greg and I grabbed a couple of wooden stools at the bar, and the bartender sized us up. We both ordered gin and tonics, and as she handed us our drinks, I caught a glimpse of a friendly but reserved smile. The man sitting to the left of me was drunk. Really drunk. As I looked around, it seemed that everyone in the bar was: bodies swayed back and forth, Bud Lights gripped in their hands. The man leaned over to me, with browning teeth and stale breath, and began to complain about the "forest circus." I told him that my father worked for the *forest service* and braced myself for a tirade as he reeled back in disgust, but Greg leaned over and soothed him. "It's okay, man, her father is old-school forest service. They were a whole different breed back then."

The bartender leaned over to the man and said affectionately, "Stop bothering these nice people, Frank. You know as well as anybody that you're full of shit."

A woman at the end of the bar, who had been eyeing Greg, leaned over and slurred, "You two are both full of shit, ya know? Who cares, anyway? I just want another drink. Why don't we all do a shot?"

Meanwhile, the bartender was pulling something very slimy and soft out of a jar. I caught a glimpse of a dirty label that read "Pickled Turkey Giblets." She threw it on a plastic plate, stuck a plastic fork in it, and pushed it over to the woman.

"Here, eat this, honey," she said. I flinched when I realized that this would be the woman's dinner. As I watched the woman slice through the giblet with her knife, I felt an ache in my chest.

There are women who succeed at life in the West, who eat oatmeal in the morning, do yoga while the sun rises, and then take the dogs for a hike in the hills. And then there are the women who fail, who make a drink for breakfast, who never see outside the dark paneling of a bar, and who actually enjoy a meal that consists of pickled giblets. I was beginning to fear that I was headed toward the latter. My eyes connected with Greg's, and he looked like he was going to gag. He motioned me to get up.

GREG AND I finally escaped and headed up the road to make camp near the hot springs. Greg went to elaborate lengths to create a tentlike construction out of the back of the truck that would allow us to view the stars, while protecting us from the rain. I laughed because I knew that he was drunk, and being ridiculous. My laughter made him happy, and he hugged me hard, his first sign of real affection all day. We walked down the road to the springs and swam, kissed, and laughed. He took a picture of me in front of the Sawtooth peaks, and I was very happy in it, full of love.

THE NEXT MORNING was a disaster. We were both cold, and Greg was hungover. It rained all night, the makeshift tent was a failure, and our stuff was soaked. Greg was giving me the silent treatment for reasons that I didn't fully understand, but I thought might have had something to do with his feelings of inadequacy as an outdoorsman. We drove down the mountain in silence.

Greg wanted to save the world. He felt so passionately about equality and socialism that he had dedicated his life to making the world better for the working class, and I loved him for this. I loved him for his big heart. Yet somehow his heart wasn't big enough for me. I always felt like a pet when I was around him, begging for love.

GREG'S SADNESS OVERWHELMED me at times, and he could be bitter or mean. Once, when he was drunk, he told me that my friends use me for the "ugly girl," and my breath caught in my throat. I didn't know what to say. "You think I'm ugly?" I asked quietly. He laughed, patting me on my shoulder.

"Oh no," he said, "but your friends are beautiful in the more mainstream way, and every group of women has to have the woman they think makes them look better. They *think* that's you, but the irony is that you're far prettier than them—just in a different way." He continued talking, but I didn't hear the words that followed. I was sitting on his couch, stunned, not sure if I had just heard a compliment or an insult. I felt sick at his cruelty, though I knew that it was the alcohol talking.

In the dark nights, when I stretched out awake beside him, I always knew that I couldn't compete with alcohol.

THE LAST SUMMER that Greg and I were together was the summer the fires started. They began at the end of June, and by July, millions of acres of forest had exploded into flame. The sky was so dark during the middle of the day that I could almost convince myself to crawl back into bed. I was beginning to feel more and more like a victim. The mood in town was bleak, and people were uncharacteristically irritable. I was reminded of the long, cold winters when the cabin fever would get so bad that fights would erupt all over town—especially bar fights. I could be sitting in a warm, cozy bar while it was ten below zero outside, and in the corner would be a mess of fists and Wrangler jeans while every cowboy within a fifty-foot radius fought to get a piece.

STILL, IN THE summer, life was usually good. The weather was warm, the skies sunny. Everybody was making money, and these same cowboys would be slapping each other on the back and sharing dips from their cans of Skoal.

But that particular summer felt more like winter. The sunlight couldn't even penetrate the layer of smoke. One day I walked to the restaurant where I worked in a white shirt, and by the time I arrived, the crisp cotton had tiny black streaks like tears streaking down it from the ash. Later, while filling salt and pepper shakers, I looked out the restaurant window. It's snowing, I thought, giddy. I started laughing and cried out for Kent, the owner, to come out from the kitchen. "Look, it's snowing. It's like a miracle."

"Well, I'll be . . . ," he said. He opened the door and stepped outside with his hands outstretched, as if in supplication. But when he stepped back into the restaurant, he was shaking his head. "It's not snow," he said. "It's ash." He held out his upturned hands, and his palms were black.

The next day at work, I was talking to Kent in the kitchen. He was chopping carrots into the shape of flowers, drinking a beer, and giving me advice while I sat on a stainless-steel cooler.

"Why would you be with someone like that?" he asked, his knife slicing through the carrots. "You're young and smart. Look, I'm just going to say it. Guys are dicks. You aren't going to change them. He isn't going to quit drinking for you. You deserve more."

I knew that Kent was right, but I didn't want to end things with Greg. I believed that love was hard work; it required sacrifice.

GREG AND I had planned to spend a weekend away together before he headed south for school. He needed to do some research at the university library in Moscow, Idaho. I had planned the trip in my head. He would go through the Frank Church Wilderness and International Workers of the World archives at the University of Idaho, while I would sit at a café and read and drink coffee. Later, we would explore the countryside and long blazing patchwork fields, tiny agricultural communities with nothing more than a grain elevator and some quiet buildings. In my head, the weekend had already happened a thousand times over.

In Moscow, Greg began to drink gin and tonics at 10:00 a.m. By 8:00 p.m., I was holding him while he cried. He was watching *Sometimes a Great Notion*. The beautiful scenes of timber and logging and men with strong forearms and sweet homemaker wives brought him to tears, great rolling sobs, and I began to feel myself cry, and looked down and realized that my shirt was wet.

"Tell me how much you love me," I said.

"I love you a lot," he said, "because you understand me." He was quiet then, and I really did understand. I curled up in his lap, and he kissed my head while I mourned and understood that we were over.

I headed home alone, feeling sad, yet somehow relieved. The fires were still burning, but I knew the snow was coming soon.

Later that week, he came to see me before returning to his home. There was a dry, windy storm raging. We drove up a winding road until we hit the top of a hill and then stood in the wind looking up at the looming black cliffs. In front us, we saw a lightning strike and then a tree blow up like a firecracker. Trees were igniting in front of us like sparklers. The fire was raging, and a swell of smoke hit my face and caught in my throat. I laid my head on Greg's shoulder as we stood on that hill and watched the trees burn. I felt that it was the last time that we would be together, but it wasn't. He broke my heart, and then he broke my heart again, and I let him. I simply did not know how to let someone go.

FINALLY, A FEW years later, I received a letter from Greg, telling me that he had quit drinking. He wrote that when he was drinking, he had been unable to appreciate my love. He wanted another chance, and I wanted to give him one. By then he lived in the midwest, and I was in Boise, but we flew to see each other. Still, although he was no longer drinking, there was a darkness inside him. I didn't know what demons he was wrestling, or how to help him, and after so many years without him, I no longer had the determination to try. When I returned to Boise, I called him and told him that I didn't want to be involved with him anymore, that my continued ties to him were keeping me from finding happiness with someone else. I didn't want to be a person who gave up on someone I had once loved, and I didn't know if I was making the right decision, but I knew that we couldn't continue. When I ended things with Greg, I felt proud—liberated. I had finally become the independent woman that I wanted to be.

I met Caleb five months after ending my tumultuous relationship with Greg. Caleb seemed so different from Greg— quieter, funnier, and kinder. As Caleb and I drove through those mountains, I thought of how Greg had pushed me to read books that I didn't want to read, made suggestions on how I should dress, encouraged me to lose weight. I knew that Caleb accepted me as I was. I knew that never—even in his darkest moments—would he call me the "ugly girl."

ON THAT AUTUMN day with Caleb, I smiled at him as we drove farther into the mountains. Dusk was falling, and we had left the main road. By then, we were farther from Atlanta and closer to the ridgeline where, only months earlier, Caleb had offered a proposal. We were already engaged, had bought the ring even, but he had said that he wanted to do the proposal right, and so he kneeled at my feet, a green, tree-dotted valley spread out behind him, and I knew that we were going to spend our lives together.

SOON CALEB TOOK a right at a fork in the road, and I grew nervous. It was a forest service road, and I could tell that it was not well traveled. "I think we should turn around," I said. "I think that we're getting lost."

"It's okay," Caleb said. "We'll just drive this road until we come out on the highway."

I looked at him, eyes widening. "It doesn't work that way with forest service roads," I said. "They don't all find their way back to the highway."

"Sure they do," he said.

I knew that he was wrong, and I could see the road ahead of us. Grass was growing in the tire ruts. "Really, Caleb, that's not the way roads work here. Maybe they're like that in West Virginia, but not in the national forest."

He slammed on the brakes. "Quit telling me what to do. I know what I'm doing!"

I shut my mouth, heart racing. My eyes teared up. I was eight months pregnant. I didn't want to get lost in the mountains. "I'm scared of getting lost," I said.

"We're not going to get lost!"

I shrunk back into my seat. "Okay," I said, my voice small.

"Quit doing that! Quit acting like you're afraid of me."

"Okay," I said again.

He started the car up again and drove forward. We were both silent. Soon the road was overtaken with grass, and it ended in a field. Caleb banged his hand on the steering wheel, then said to me—his voice hard—"Don't even say it. I don't want to hear it." He turned the car around and headed back the way we had come. We rode in silence, and I was relieved when we came back onto the main road. He stopped along the way, obviously still angry with me. He opened his door. "You stay here," he said, "I have to shoot my gun. It's loaded."

"Okay," I said, staring out the window.

He went around to the back of the car, but then came to my side of the car and knocked on my door. I opened it, and he took my hand in his. His eyes were gentle, almost frightened. "I'm sorry," he said. "If anything happens to me, I want you to know that I love you."

"Why would anything happen to you?" I asked.

"It's my muzzle-loader," he said. "It's jammed."

"What does that mean?" I asked. "Is it going to backfire on you? Wait, are you afraid that you're going to die?"

He patted my hand, but I could tell that he was nervous. "I'll be fine," he said. "I just wanted to tell you that I love you."

He went to the back of the vehicle, and soon I heard the loud crack of the muzzle-loader. I jumped, involuntarily squinting my eyes shut. I didn't open them again until the driver's door opened; then my muscles relaxed, and I leaned over to rest my head on Caleb's shoulder. He hugged me tightly. "That was close," he said.

I was scared, and also furious that he had brought a loaded weapon into the car with him, particularly when it was a weapon that hadn't been cleaned and might have misfired. Still, more than that, I was relieved that he was okay. "I'm sorry that I told you what to do," I said.

"It's okay. You're pregnant, and you're scared. That's what I love about you. I love how much you care about our baby." He squeezed me tighter, then let go and started the car.

I was relieved that he was alive. Maybe even more than that, I was relieved that he was no longer angry at me. I could breathe again. As we drove through the dark forest, then pulled out onto the highway, I realized that my expressions of concern had felt like criticism to him. I knew that I could be overly critical; Greg had said the same thing about me, and he, too, had so often been angry with me. As we headed home, winding up a mountain pass that would then dip us back into the Boise Valley, I held Caleb's hand, grateful for his forgiveness.

7

I Love You

WHEN THE BABY came, the moon was high and full in the dark night sky. My due date had come and gone ten days earlier, and after following an old wives' tale and drinking as much red raspberry leaf tea as my stomach could hold, my water broke. I took a shower and let the water run over me—watched the shampoo suds mix with my amniotic fluid and circle the drain. I pictured myself as an egg that had cracked.

I wasn't scared.

MY PARENTS HAD come to help, but when my due date came and went, my father had to return home to work. My mother stayed on with Caleb and me, and she cleaned our house, organized our shelves, bought us food to have in the fridge. She took me to the store and purchased a rug for the baby's room, bright yellow, along with a wall-hanging clock of a cheery-looking monkey whose tail swung in a tick-tock, tick-tock.

My in-laws had offered to buy bedding for Reed's crib, and I had struggled to find something that I liked. I didn't want a crib set. The expense seemed excessive to me when we only had a small amount of money in our bank account. I would rather have had something practical, but my mother-in-law pushed me. "Surely you want something cute for the baby's room?" she said. "Surely the baby deserves that?" There was a hint of criticism in her voice. It was a criticism that I had become accustomed to in the brief time that I had known her.

WHEN I WAS around my mother-in-law, Joanne, I drowned in her kindness—it was a kindness that I didn't ask for, and a kindness that asked for much in return. When I tried to explain it to Kelly M., she told me, "Oh honey, I had a southern grandma. You will never out*nice* a southern woman." It seemed that Kelly M. was right, so I usually bit my tongue and went along with Joanne's desires, but I grew to resent her.

When I expressed my frustration to Caleb, his response was always exasperated. I think that he, too, was fatigued by her. I think that he had moved across the country as a way of asserting his independence from his mother.

"She won't let me ignore her," I said. "I already have a controlling mother. I don't really enjoy having another one."

"I know," he said, and he did, but still, he didn't know what to do about it. I was tired at that point and had developed pregnancy-induced hypertension. My ob-gyn had put me on a modified bed rest. "You're too stressed," she said. "Maybe you should try drinking a beer every night to relax. This kind of stress isn't good for the baby."

I tried to relax, but the phone rang multiple times a day. I usually let the answering machine pick up, but there would

be a hang-up, and then it would ring again, the caller ID always Joanne's.

I asked Caleb to tell his mother to stop calling if we didn't
answer the first time, but I think he was afraid of her. He
said that she *punished* him when he asked for things. I sometimes wondered if he had moved into Idaho City, where he
had no cell service, just to escape his mother's constant calls.
The phone kept ringing, and my fatigue and exasperation in-
creased.

The first time Joanne and I spoke on the phone, I had not
yet met her in person, but I was already engaged to Caleb.
She and my father-in-law, Charles, had offered to buy us a set
of pots and pans as our wedding gift. I loved to cook and was
excited about the gift. Caleb had sent his mother a link to the
set of pots and pans that I wanted.

"Oh no," Joanne said to me on the phone. "We're going to
buy you the same pots and pans that we have. They're very
good."

I hesitated. "I don't really know how to cook on stainless-
steel pots and pans," I said. "And they're the same price as
the other ones, so . . ."

She was silent, then said firmly, "You'll like the ones we're
ordering for you. Charles and I love ours."

She was warm and kind, but I had already been overwhelmed by her demands for our wedding. I felt that I was
being pulled along on a current I couldn't resist.

"Okay," I conceded. After all, how could I object to a gift?
What kind of terrible person would that make me?

At the end of our phone conversation, she said, "I love you," and I faltered.

I didn't know how to say it back.

"Thank you," I replied. I heard silence on her end. I could hear her hurt feelings in that silence. I hung up the phone. Why had I been so stingy with that phrase? Why was it so difficult for me to say it? I remembered the first time I heard Caleb tell his mother on the phone that he loved her, and how that had endeared him to me by proving that he wasn't ice but all warmth. I remembered how I had craved that kind of warmth with my own family, where we never said "I love you" to each other.

I REMEMBERED HOW, when I told Greg that I loved him, it meant we would be together forever. I remembered how safe those words had felt to me then, how liberally our conversations were peppered with the word *love*.

I remembered how naive I was.

AFTER GREG, I had told myself that I would never say those words first to a man again, and then I dated the fish biologist. He was kinder to me than any man had ever been. I loved him, and his kindness made me feel that he loved me too. Still, he didn't say the words. I waited. Finally, I started pushing. "I feel like I want to have more of a commitment," I said.

He looked at me, then said, "Are you talking about the l-word?" I didn't reply, but the answer was obvious. "I'm not going to say that until I want to marry someone," he said.

A couple of months later he turned to me, just as I was falling asleep, "I love you," he whispered in my ear. I jerked awake, unsure of what to say.

"What did you say?" I asked. I wanted to be sure.

He tensed up. "Nothing."

"No, tell me what you said," I begged.

"It was nothing," he said again. I gave up and rolled over.

I returned to Boise for school, and soon a card arrived in my mailbox. In it, he had written, "I know that being in a long-distance relationship is hard, but I also know that it will be worth it in the end. I love you."

I stood there in the street reading that card. *He loved me.*

I was worth loving.

A COUPLE OF weeks later, I returned to Salmon for the summer. I was so excited to see him, but also a little nervous about the turn that our relationship had taken. I went to his house, where he made me dinner. We watched television and cuddled on the couch, but then, without warning, he told me that he didn't think we could see each other anymore. "I was looking at you tonight, and I kept thinking to myself, Do I love her? And I don't think that I do," he said.

I walked home to my parents' house, sick, went into the backyard, and broke into tears. My mother, although usually reserved, came out and held me. "I had a feeling that something was wrong," she said. "I'm so sorry."

"You don't understand," I said. "You married Dad when you were twenty-one. You've never had your heart broken."

"You don't know everything about me," she said. Her face was sad too. "I thought that you and he were going to make it," she said. "I always knew that you were safe with him."

A COUPLE OF days later, he called me and asked me to go for a walk. On our walk, he said, "I talked to my mom. She thinks that I'm just scared. She thinks that I made the wrong decision. I don't want to make the wrong decision."

We went back to his apartment and made love. It was intense, angry, and afterward, when he collapsed on top of me, I started sobbing. It was clear that I wasn't worth loving.

"Oh, Kelly," he said, rolling over and gathering me into his arms.

"I hate you," I said.

"I know," he replied.

A COUPLE OF years after the fish biologist broke my heart, on the same cold night in Idaho City that Cory danced with Kelly M., Caleb played the guitar at a bar with a band called Last Man Standing. With the exception of Caleb, they were a group of men in their sixties who had chosen their band name because all but one had experienced a heart attack. Caleb was only twenty-four, but those men treated him with such respect. Everyone in his life adored him.

He played the guitar and sang directly to me. His blue eyes glowed, and so did mine.

Cory slid into a seat next to me. "I've never seen a woman look at Caleb like that," he joked. "What's wrong with you?"

I smiled at Cory. "I like him," I said.

Cory leaned in closer, his eyes serious, "The other day, Caleb and I were driving around in the mountains, and we were listening to the mix CD that you made him for Christmas. He told me that he thinks he's in love with you. He thinks you're the person he wants to marry."

I wasn't surprised. Cory may have never seen a woman look at Caleb like that, but I'd also never seen a man look at me like Caleb looked at me.

That night, I curled up next to Caleb in his warm cabin. "Cory says that you think I'm the one," I teased. I knew that Caleb would be annoyed—that the conversation had been private—and as usual, Cory had been drinking.

"Cory is stupid," he said.

"So it's not true?" I asked.

"I didn't say that," he said, leaning in to kiss me. His beard tickled my neck. I wrapped my arms and legs around him.

LESS THAN A year later, I was standing over the kitchen stove, crying. My pregnant belly butted up against the metal stove.

"What is wrong with you?" Caleb asked.

I pointed at the pan, an egg stuck to the metal, dried out and burned. "I don't know how to cook with these pans," I said.

"For fuck's sake, Kelly! It's just an egg."

I was embarrassed at my reaction. "I know," I said.

"Just get out of here," he said. "I'll make you an egg. I

obviously have to do everything for you." Then he screamed, "Stop crying!"

I cried louder.

I WENT TO the living room and sat numbly on the couch. I heard him crack an egg into the pan, then in a few moments, he shouted "F-u-u-u-c-k!" I jumped. My family had never used language like that.

I heard him scraping the egg into the trash, then another egg cracked into the pan. A few minutes later, he came out with a plate with an egg and toast. He was calm. "Here," he said gently. "I'm sorry. Those pans are the worst."

I started laughing. "They really are," I said. Caleb started laughing, too, and soon we were both doubled over.

"I'll go buy a cheap pan at a thrift store, just for eggs."

I smiled at him, my face still red and puffy from tears. "Okay," I replied. "That's a good idea."

WHEN THE BABY came, he split me in two. I screamed at the final moment, as the yellow line on the monitor reached its peak, and then my flesh ripped. Relief. The baby slipped onto the table, slick and red. And crying. Was I crying? I can't remember. I remember Caleb crying. And smiling. The nurse brought the baby to my breast, laid his skin against mine. Caleb couldn't stop crying.

Caleb later told me that when he saw the pain I was in, he couldn't stand it. He knew things about himself that I didn't know yet. He wanted to tell me. There was so much he wanted to tell me. He was so, so sorry.

But I didn't know any of this while my baby rooted at my chest. I only knew Caleb's eyes, so full of love and hope, and something that also looked like guilt, but I didn't yet know what his guilt was about.

When the baby came, I was twenty-seven years old, and Caleb was twenty-five. Only a few weeks before, Caleb had come home from drinking with Cory at a nearby bar. He crawled into bed with me, then began to shake. "Caleb," I said, pushing him on the shoulder. He shook more, but didn't say anything. "Caleb," I begged, my voice growing panicked. He turned and vomited on the bed. I heaved myself out of bed, my belly so large, then dragged him up and to the bathroom. He vomited into the toilet while I stood in the doorway and watched.

When he was finished, he stumbled into the bedroom and stared at the bed, still too drunk to understand what he had done. I walked him to the couch, where he curled into a ball, then went back to the bedroom, bundled up the dirty sheets, and walked them to the basement of our apartment building, where I threw them into the washer. I took a rag and some dish soap and scrubbed the mattress. I gagged. The baby kicked in response to my gagging, and I held my hand to the shape of his outstretched foot.

I went to the living room, turned Caleb on his side, and felt his chest to make sure that he was breathing. He whimpered like a child, and I smoothed my hand over his forehead. I slept on the hardwood floor that night.

THE NEXT DAY, Caleb was more apologetic than I had ever seen him. He told me that Cory had kept ordering pitchers of beer, and that Caleb hadn't known how to say no. Cory had dropped Caleb off at our house, then driven all the way home to Idaho City. Years later, Cory would get his fourth or fifth DUI and go to prison for a year. When he was released from prison, he would write Caleb and apologize. He would tell Caleb that he was sorry, and that he knew that he, Cory, hadn't treated me right, but I didn't know any of that when the baby came.

I only knew that I had already loved an alcoholic once, and that I couldn't do it again. Caleb promised me that he wouldn't drink like that again, but it was difficult for me to believe him. Greg hadn't been able to change for me, and even if he had, I don't think that he had loved me enough to try. Still, I had to believe that Caleb was different.

A WEEK LATER, Caleb's friend who had helped us move came over and made us dinner. He set up a table in the yard and cooked lamb and spring pea soup. I was happy to be included. None of our close friends had children, and I had been feeling excluded. Caleb's friend had bought an expensive bottle of wine, and I had a sip from Caleb's glass. I told his friend the story of Caleb coming home the week before and vomiting in the bed. I laughed. "Can you believe that?" I said.

The friend put his wine down, got quiet. "I don't think that story is very funny," he said.

I thought about it for a moment. I thought about how terrible and scared I had felt when Caleb had shaken in our bed.

I thought about how it had only taken me a week to turn the story into a joke.

"You're right," I said quietly. "It's not very funny."

WHEN THE BABY came, my mother was in the delivery room with us. My blood pressure had crashed after an epidural. Caleb held my hand, and I saw him receding into the distance. "I feel funny," I heard myself whisper before sinking into darkness. I came back to consciousness when the anesthesiologist stuck a needle of ephedrine in me.

When I woke, my mother's face was at the foot of the bed. She, too, looked ready to pass out.

"I'm sorry," I whimpered. I apologized to the nurse, to my mother, to Caleb. I thought that I was failing at childbirth, just as I had failed at everything else.

The ephedrine made my heart race. The nurse said that my heart rate was so fast that I might as well have been running a marathon, and I was sweating, so I shed my hospital gown. The nurse brought in a big fan. Caleb had his coat and snow hat on, shivering from the cold blast.

"I'm sorry," I whispered again.

He smoothed my damp hair back from my head. "You're doing great," he said. "You're amazing." He started to cry. "I love you," he said.

"I love you too," I said through my tears.

WHEN THE BABY came, the nurse brought him to my chest. He latched on to my breast, and my toes curled from the pain. No one had told me that it would hurt like that. The baby started sucking, and his little hand, which had been curled into a fist, relaxed.

We named him Reed after Caleb's grandfather. I looked up at Caleb and smiled, "In the ultrasound, I thought that he looked like you, but he looks just like me," I said.

Caleb laughed, face still teary. "That's a good thing," he said. "He's beautiful just like his mama."

WE SPENT THE next two days in the hospital, and my mother was there the entire time. With her help, I didn't feel scared, but when the nurse wheeled me out of the hospital, I held Reed bundled up in my arms, and while he slept peacefully, tears dripped down my cheeks. I didn't understand where they were coming from. I felt nothing. No sadness, and no fear.

My mother looked at me with a gentleness that seemed to understand.

"It looks like someone has the baby blues," she said.

WE WENT HOME, and my father came to join us. I didn't want my parents to ever leave, but they couldn't stay. Their departure overlapped with my in-laws' arrival, which made me miss my own parents even more. Joanne was so happy to see and hold Reed, and she was equally happy to see Caleb, but the tension between the two of us was palpable. I didn't want to be one of those mothers who didn't let other people hold her baby, but when Reed was happy, she always wanted to hold him. She only let me have him when he cried. She and Charles were uncomfortable watching me nurse, so at least I could escape with Reed to the nursery, where I spent most of my time cloistered away with my very hungry baby.

When Kelly M. and her younger sister came over to visit, they came with me to the other room to nurse. I self-consciously pulled out my breast. Kelly M.'s sister looked on curiously. "Can I watch?" she asked.

"Sure," I said.

"That is so cool," she said. "I've never seen that before."

"It is pretty cool," I said, looking down at Reed's peaceful face. With my friends, I felt free of the shame.

AFTER A WEEK had passed, my in-laws left, and Caleb, Reed, and I were alone. Reed slept in a little basket on the floor by the bed, and when he cried, Caleb would pick him up and lay him next to me to nurse. Once, so that Caleb could sleep, I took Reed into his nursery to nurse him in the rocking chair.

I rocked back and forth, and felt my milk let down, my toes uncurl. It no longer hurt as much. I smoothed my hand over Reed's hair. He was a redhead like me. He was already such a good baby. I had worried that I wouldn't like being a mother, but in that moment, I didn't want anything else. I looked around that room trying to memorize all the details. I focused on the tick-tock of that monkey clock, the little tail swinging back and forth. I focused on Reed's weight in my arms. I wanted to remember that moment forever so when I felt as though I had made the wrong decision in marrying Caleb, I would have it to return to. I leaned down and touched my lips to Reed's warm forehead, his soft hair. "I love you," I whispered.

8

Demolition

WHEN SUMMER CAME around, Reed was a happy, chubby six-month-old, and Caleb and I were out of work. I was still trying to finish my undergraduate degree, and Caleb would be entering the third year of his MFA program that fall. In the meantime, we needed to pay the rent. We decided to move to Salmon, where we could live in my parents' basement and work for the forest service while my mom watched our son.

The intense scrutiny in the small town where I had grown up rattled us both. We both worked in the same office as my father, and our public and private lives merged. We fought that summer in the claustrophobic wood-paneled basement—painful, drawn-out fights in hushed voices.

Caleb worked on a timber-marking crew, and I worked sampling streams. Timber marking was relatively easy work—hiking and spray-painting X's on trees that would need to be cut down—but stream sampling was hard. I had to sit in the middle of cold mountain streams and dig buckets of rocks out of the hard creek beds. At the beginning of the season my arms were so sore that when I got home in the evenings to find Reed's little arms outstretched toward mine, I could barely lift him. Caleb always rushed

to the basement when we got to the house, leaving me upstairs alone with my parents with Reed's tender weight in
my heavy arms.

Still, being at my parents' house meant that we had consistent babysitters, which was something we hadn't had in
Boise, and I was determined to enjoy that. Having babysitters meant that we could go to events like the demolition
derby, the biggest event of the year in Salmon.

The derby took place during Salmon River Days, a four-
day festival of sidewalk sales, parades, and what passed
in my town for pageantry. The 4-H kids led their animals
down Main Street, and the cheerleaders rode on the backs of
trucks, but the rodeo queens were the stars. They rode their
horses with draping satin banners, bedazzled in pinks and
blues, tall cowboy hats perched on their heads. The horses
ambled and swung while the rodeo queens, with coiffed
hair and perfect teeth, smiled and waved. Behind them, an
adolescent boy rode a four-wheeler, quickly cleaning up the
horseshit by efficiently sweeping it into a bucket.

Finally, at the end of the parade, we got what we were
waiting for: the line of demolition-derby cars. They had
been painted by amateurs, but the brightly colored doors
and animal-print backgrounds had character. Each car was
covered in advertisements for local businesses, such as the
Savage Circle, a fast-food stand. On the side of their squat
building, underneath the picture of an Indian chief (the
same as the high school mascot), in large black letters, the
Savage Circle motto read: "We Use 100% Beef (Except for

the Chicken)." There were no corporate chains in Salmon except for the Subway sandwich shop, which had opened when I was in high school.

I thrilled at the sight of the loud derby cars, the roar of the engines, and the ladies perched on the hoods. It quickly became my favorite yearly event—an affirmation of the culture I had been raised in. There was a tension in Salmon—an undercurrent of despair fueled by boredom and poverty. This underbelly was inescapable, written in the faces of my classmates, in the subtext of every conversation. Always, it was most evident in the reunion that took place at the derby, when the residents of Salmon—both past and present— came together to celebrate the smashing of cars.

Spectators packed the bleachers; bare legs vied for space with plastic cushions that farted out the smell of old closets. On the horizon loomed the Beaverhead Mountains, a row of jagged peaks, still snowcapped in July. Salmon is a town of contradictions, of hippies and back-to-landers living next to ranchers and loggers. Still, the vast open space creates an inescapable loneliness in most, and the demolition derby becomes a cathartic ritual of violence and destruction.

Just as the cars began to rev their engines, I caught a glimpse of Jeannie, Jay, and Bud, and waved them over. Caleb gave me a quick smile, relieved to see someone he knew. Whenever we went out in Salmon, he was forced to endure small talk with strangers. A trip to the grocery store involved five or six conversations in which I introduced Caleb, talked about the baby, and issued general updates on my life. Once, after a particularly grueling grocery-store visit, Caleb let out a sigh of relief in the car and said, "You could be the mayor of Salmon. You know everyone."

Caleb was nervous at the derby. He had spent time with Jeannie and Jay, so he was comfortable with them, but Jeannie was bringing along her father, Bud, who could be a difficult man. They all climbed the bleacher steps and came to sit next to us. I scooted over to make room. I introduced Caleb to Bud, then turned to give Jeannie a hug. She pulled me close and whispered in my ear that Bud's wife had left him, moved to Montana, and become a lesbian.

I looked back at Bud. It was over a hundred degrees, and he was still wearing wool, a plaid shirt. His beard was dark and full. He caught me looking at him and glowered. "What are *you* looking at, Red?" He had called me Red since I was a child, a nickname I didn't appreciate.

I turned back to Jeannie and said, "Pretty ironic."

SHORTLY AFTER JEANNIE and I became friends, fifteen years earlier, she had invited me to her house for a barbecue. Bud opened the door. Unlike my father, a gentle, sober church-going man, Bud was a logger who loved to go to bars and get rowdy with the guys. He wore red plaid shirts and suspenders, and had a long though neatly trimmed beard. He was a walking parody of a lumberjack—big and brawny—and when he occasionally strutted around the house shirtless, his shoulders and chest were covered in black hair. When I grew older, I jokingly called him a yeti behind his back.

That night, as he accompanied me through the den to-ward the backyard, the eyes of a mountain lion followed me from a stone perch mounted on the wall. The den had rough-hewn log walls, and in addition to the mountain lion, there was a stuffed musk ox, a wolverine, various elk and deer heads, and a polar-bear skin proudly hanging over the full bar. Bud was an avid trophy hunter, and the house was like an animal mausoleum, where the faint smell of turpentine and death mingled with the smell of vodka and Bud Light.

Bud was a smart man—with a good heart at his core—but he was a "man's man," whatever that meant to him.

THE ANNOUNCER SCREAMED out over the loudspeaker, "Aaaall right, Salmon. Are you ready to git 'er done?" We swiveled to watch the action as the cars began pulling out into the mud. The engines growled as the tires spun. Each car paraded around the course, spewing as much mud into the air as possible.

When the cars slid into their places in the starting circle, the drivers climbed out the driver-side windows (the doors were welded shut) and raised their arms for applause. The drivers were mostly men; they spent the entire year souping up their engines, reinforcing the doors with bars, and replac-ing the windows with metal grates. A great deal of pride and money went into the competition, and in Salmon, pride and money are in short supply.

The derby ran in ten long heats, including the Motorcycle

Heat, the Powder Puff Heat (for lady drivers), and the Herby Derby.

As the cars revved their engines to begin, one of the drivers leaned out and flipped the crowd off. We went wild.

ONCE THE FIRST heat was ready, Judge Snyder bullhorned, "Get ready and start your engines!" The engines roared, and the drivers careened toward the middle of the course, bouncing off each other in the frenzy.

As Judge Snyder hooted at the drivers, Jeannie leaned over and shouted in my ear, "Do you remember traffic court?"

I laughed and turned to tell the story to Caleb. We had been fourteen—observing traffic court for our driver's education class—and I was surprised to hear Judge Snyder offer three pleas to defendants: guilty, not guilty, and guilty with an excuse. When a sobbing woman pleaded "guilty with an excuse" to a DUI charge, Judge Snyder nodded.

"Very well," he said. "What's your excuse?"

"Well," the woman said, "I was almost to my house. I had made it all the way to the turn before the cop pulled me over. I normally wouldn't have been out drinking, but my husband had just divorced me . . ." She started sniffling a little bit more and looked down, wiping her nose on her sleeve. When she looked back up, she said, "I just didn't know what to do."

Judge Snyder said, "It looks like you had a good excuse. I'll drop the charges this time, but don't do it again."

Bud interrupted my story. "Well, at least her husband didn't leave her to move to Missoula and munch box."

We fell silent. I looked down at the action below, just in time to see the front end of a car crumpled back into its windshield.

When we didn't respond, he spoke again, louder. "You give your whole life to someone, and then they leave you to become a box muncher."

Our silence was uncomfortable, so Caleb nodded and smiled at Bud out of politeness, but when he looked at me, his face registered horror.

When Bud looked away, I mouthed to Caleb: *I warned you.*

THE FIRST HEAT was in full swing now, and the audience was energized. Each driver still hoped for victory. In the first heat, everyone felt like a winner.

The drivers' strategies became obvious fairly quickly. The driver of car 16, sponsored by a windshield-repair place, drove into the middle of the ring and began aggressively ramming any car that came within ten feet. His bumper got hooked on the bumper of car 7, sponsored by Langer Distributing, with the words "I Love U, Barb" spray-painted over a graphic of a Pepsi can.

Both cars' tires spun uselessly as they tried to separate, engines squealing, steam bubbling out from underneath the hoods. Soon the other drivers saw 16's vulnerability, and he became a target. Five cars took turns exacting their vengeance, slamming into him with painful crunches. There was only one rule in the derby. One car couldn't slam into another's driver-side door. Beyond that, it was a free-for-all.

Together, the cars slammed 16 free from 7's bumper, and then 7 took his turn slamming 16. Soon, smoke was pouring out from underneath 16's hood. A siren went off, and the other cars pulled away. They drove to the edges of the ring, idling, while the driver clambered out his window. The fire department sprayed the car as the driver stood by, shoulders slumped, watching. When they finished putting out the fire, he climbed back in the window, reached his arm out, and pulled down his red flag.

When the siren sounded again, the other cars raced back into the ring and spun in circles. One driver tried to play it safe. He circled the action, avoiding the other cars. At one point, he idled quietly in a corner, clearly hoping the other drivers wouldn't notice him, but hiding wasn't a good strategy. They backed him into the corner. It only took three good hits, metal upon metal, before he reached out and pulled down his flag.

Jeannie leaned over and tapped my knee. "Seventeen is Ginny," she said. "She skipped the Powder Puff. That takes guts. The derby is a good ol' boys club."

I smiled at the mud flying from Ginny's wheels as her car ripped around a corner. Ginny and I had been in school together. We had a brief friendship in grade school—even going so far as to prick our fingers with a needle and rub the fleshy tips together while waiting for the school bus. Blood sisters, we called it—our blood forever merged. By high school, our lives were different, and I hadn't spoken to her in years.

While Jeannie and I talked, Caleb was forced to visit with Jay and Bud. Having grown up in Appalachia, Caleb was no stranger to men like Bud, but Caleb also knew that those kinds of men made me uncomfortable. I looked back and smiled to reassure Caleb that I was okay—I was used to Bud. He reached out and squeezed my shoulder. I patted his hand, comforted by his tenderness. Jeannie leaned over and tapped my knee. "Let's go get a cheeseburger," she said.

I nodded and stood up. I turned back to Caleb. "We're going to get a cheeseburger," I said. "Do you want anything?" Caleb nodded and said a beer would be great.

Jay laughed and punched Caleb in the arm. "Aah, you guys are newlyweds," he said. "She still does things like get you cheeseburgers. That won't last."

Jeannie shrugged when I looked back at Caleb; his face was puzzled. "I think she'll always buy me cheeseburgers," he said, slowly.

"Sure I will," I said. I was confused. My parents still did things for each other after thirty-five years of marriage. "Why should that change?" I asked Jay.

Jeannie and Jay were the experts on all things marriage. They seemed so meant for each other that when I was with them, I could believe that marriage was sweet and earnest— that it wasn't hard. Before Jay had the chance to answer, Jeannie grabbed my arm and pulled me away. "At least she's not in Missoula . . . ," Bud said.

I bristled, ready to tell him off. Still, when I looked at him, I stopped. He was staring at the cars demolishing each other down below, his face wooden, his eyes sparkling in the sunlight as he fought back tears. He was obviously in pain. For all of his puffing, I could tell that he missed his wife. I turned around, acting like I hadn't heard him.

I hurried to catch up to Jeannie, who was standing at the bottom of the bleachers talking to a high school buddy, a woman who'd been impregnated at nineteen by the star point guard on the basketball team.

I waited silently while Jeannie finished talking to her friend. As we were walking off, I brought the conversation back to Jay.

"What was that all about with Jay?"

Jeannie looked away and then looked back. "You guys are newbies," she said. "You don't get it yet. In the beginning, you do all of these things for each other, because you're so in love, and you want to. But after a while, you don't want to do things for each other anymore. I mean, why should you?"

"You're right," I said. "I don't get that."

She sighed. "You spend your whole life trying to figure out who does more, who works more, who takes care of the kids more, and who does more in bed. I mean, look at me," she said. She stood back and held out her arms. She had become frail. Her body, already small, was now tiny. I couldn't believe I hadn't noticed it before.

"I've lost forty pounds," she said. "I'm a size zero now. Sometimes I have to buy my clothing in the children's section. I lost all of this weight, because I thought it was what he wanted, but he still doesn't want me. If there is nothing I can do to make him happy, why should I try?"

I stood there, stunned. I didn't know what to say.

When we reached the counter of the brew-pub kiosk, Jeannie ordered a cheeseburger and a beer. I ordered two beers. She patted my shoulder. "Hey, lighten up," she said. "I don't want you to think we're having problems or anything. We're fine. It just happens to all couples. You get used to it."

"Okay," I said. I was afraid of what might come next and changed the subject. "How many more times do you think Judge Snyder will say 'Git 'er done'?"

Jeannie laughed and squirted some ketchup on her burger. "I don't know," she said, then took a bite. "Maybe we should turn that into the Judge Snyder Meets Larry the Cable Guy drinking game."

When we reached our seats, Bud and Jay were talking quietly. Caleb looked left out. We had more room on our bench, so I patted the seat next to me, and he squeezed in beside me. I handed him his beer, and he popped the top and smiled at me. "You missed the last heat," he said.

I shrugged and smiled. "They go on a little long anyway."

"The motorcycle round is next," he said. Unlike the derby, the motorcycle round had partners—a driver and a passenger. Each passenger had a balloon taped on a helmet and carried a Wiffle bat. The goal was to beat the balloons off the opposing teams' helmets. The last team left with a balloon won a keg of beer.

We sat and sipped our beer while the motorcycles circled.

The passenger had to grip the driver tightly so he wouldn't fall off the bike. Everyone cheered when a balloon was popped. Finally only two bikes were left on the field. They drove in circles, the passengers stretching out to hit the balloons, then pulling back. Just when it seemed as though there would be no winner, the passengers jumped off the backs of the bikes. They ran into the middle of the ring and started beating at each other's helmets wildly. Everyone cheered. I felt the violence acutely. If a balloon didn't burst, if something didn't break, I didn't know what would happen.

Finally, after what seemed like hours, one man knocked the other man's bat onto the ground. The first man stood poised, bat raised; the other man froze, his hands held up in surrender. I leaned forward, my hands gripping my knees. The man with the bat slowly lowered his weapon. He leaned down, picked up the other man's bat, then tossed it to him with a smile. I jumped out of my seat and whooped, then quickly sat back down with an embarrassed smile.

The men chuckled before resuming the fight. Finally, one of them popped the other's balloon. The winners hopped back on their bike and roared around the ring in a victory lap, swinging the Wiffle bat in a large arc in the air. Judge Snyder yelled, "Git 'er done!" Jeannie and I looked at each other and smiled. We clinked our cans and each took a drink of beer.

THE SUN WAS setting behind the mountains, red and purple splashed behind the peaks. Stars hung in a silvery veil

over the valley, shrouded by the bright lights of the arena.
The night air felt cool as we waited for the Herby Derby, my
favorite heat. I leaned in close to Caleb for warmth, and he
draped his arm around my shoulder. The cars roared into the
ring, spitting mud into the air, flying wildly in circles, but
this time they were compact cars like Toyota Corollas and
Honda Civics. The engines were not as large, and everything
felt smaller in scale.

I thought about the 1984 Toyota Camry that had driven
me through my adolescent years. It had even driven Jeannie,
Jay, and me down from a mountain hot spring when we were
nineteen. Jay had been driving, and he took a corner too fast,
skidding into a rock slide. When he stopped, Jeannie and I
got out and started moving rocks together. A fat moon hung
above us. My hair was still wet from the hot spring. "You're
so lucky," I said. "You've met this wonderful person, and I've
never even had a boyfriend."

Jeannie smiled at me as we moved a boulder together,
rolling it to the side of the road. "I know things," she said.
"And I know that you're going to meet someone wonderful,
and he is going to adore you."

She had so much faith in her own prediction that I believed her. I hugged her, and years later, when Caleb and I
went out with Jeannie and Jay for our first double date, Jeannie took me into the bathroom and said, "He is the one."

WHEN THE WINNER'S heat began, Ginny was competing
for the championship. When I ran into Ginny in town, she

seemed happy. She never complained about her marriage, and she looked at her husband with so much love in her eyes. I craved this victory for her. I wanted things to work out for someone. For anyone.

I watched her slam into the hood of a car. She quickly backed up and purposefully hit the car on the front side, setting it into a spin. The other car's tires spun as it tried to get away from her, but she continued to batter it. I admired her aggression, her confidence. The savagery was cathartic.

My hometown seemed to hold so much hidden anger, so many relationships strained by years of disillusion. I gripped Caleb's hand, knowing that relationships come to an end, that nothing is certain, but not wanting to let go.

Jeannie and Jay sat away from each other, only occasionally speaking. Bud's body was tight with anger, but I hadn't forgotten his tears. I whispered "Go, go, go" to Ginny as she continued the fight. She didn't back down. She edged the last car into a corner, but before she could hit it, the driver quickly reached out and pulled down his flag in surrender.

The crowd erupted into cheers as Ginny jumped out the window, holding her arms up in victory. I held my arms up, too, my hand still gripping Caleb's. He looked at me, confused by my excitement. I smiled at him. "I know that woman."

BUT WAIT. I missed something.

Months before the demolition derby, there was a different day. Caleb and I argued. I was in bed, and I turned my head to the wall. Squinted my eyes shut. Then I heard something guttural. Angry. "Don't cry!" he screamed. He stood up and grabbed the computer desk chair, which was heavy and on wheels. He held it above his head, and I shrank back into the covers, shaking. He heaved the chair at the wall, cracking the plaster and narrowly missing me before it fell on to the mattress by my feet.

Not since Danny had chased me with his knife, not since that man had sat in his idling truck, not since that other man had held his hand over my mouth, had I known how it felt to shake from the inside. When I turned to look at him, Caleb's eyes had never looked so cold.

That hole in the plaster formed a half-moon above our bed. At night, when my body curled into his, and we formed our own half-moon, the hole watched over me like a twisted sentry. It told me that I was not safe. Caleb never had to say a word.

9

That Hot, Dry Summer

THAT HOT, DRY summer was the summer that I spent digging in clear, cold mountain streams. The first scoop of dirt was always the easiest, the soil breaking away from the rocks, but as the holes got deeper, the soil was more packed. There were often large boulders in my way that I had to work around. I sat on that bucket, dug, and daydreamed about the things I couldn't have. Caleb was beginning to feel like one of those boulders.

THAT HOT, DRY summer I worked with a twenty-two-year-old man named Ben. He had just graduated from college with an engineering degree, and his life seemed full of possibility. I was only six years older than he, but it felt more like twenty. My life, as a wife and a mother, had aged me. I liked Ben. We drove for hours each day to the streams, and inside our work truck we were rarely silent. Ben was puzzled that I was still an undergraduate, and I didn't quite know how to explain it—that I had never fully committed to anything, that I had been uprooting myself constantly in search of something better, that for the first time in my life, I couldn't uproot myself because I had a baby who depended on me and a husband who loved me.

ONE DAY I told Ben, "I think I'll go to law school." I was in the passenger seat, and he wound the truck around a corner on a steep mountain road near the Montana border. "I need to find a way to support my family. Caleb's MFA isn't going to do it."

Ben said, "You should do that. You're smart enough to be a lawyer."

My early years of perfectionism, anxiety, and wanderlust hadn't served my GPA well, but I was determined to change. I had gone back to school when Reed was six weeks old. My breasts heavy with breast milk, I would come home to his hungry screams. Still, I maintained my 4.0. Mothering had given me a new sense of focus.

We would reach our stream for the day, get out of the truck, and pull on our thigh-high rubber waders. "Do you want to dig or sift?" Ben would ask. Sifting, which was done on the bank, was physically easier but required an attention to detail that I didn't want to have.

"Dig," I said. I liked the challenge of digging. I liked being able to lose myself in daydreams, and by then, I thought I knew how to work my way around the boulders.

THE LAST TIME that I had worked for the forest service, three years earlier, was as a wilderness river guard at a backcountry guard station, Indian Creek, in the Frank Church River of No Return Wilderness. There I lived in a tiny, electricity-free wooden cabin only accessible by backcountry plane. At that time I had been reading a lot of Edward Abbey, and I'd gone into the wilderness to be reborn through solitude. I wanted to learn how to transform my loneliness into the ever-elusive solitude that Abbey wrote about so compellingly. I kept waiting for God to speak to me from the rocks. And sometimes, when I sat very still—the wind ruffling my hair—I heard the beginnings of a voice, but it was only my own. God was silent on all counts.

Before I left for Indian Creek, Megan called. Our parents still lived one block from each other, and we were both home visiting. When I walked into her house, her mother Mary was lying on the couch under an afghan, watching *Law & Order*. She raised her hand and smiled—a weak smile. "How's the University of Montana?" she asked.

I smiled back, that kind of false smile that people use on the dying. "Oh, I'm not in Montana anymore."

Megan had just walked in from the hall. "Mom, Kelly's in Boise now," she said.

Mary closed her eyes. "Oh, right," she said. "Boise."

That day—the day before I left for Indian Creek—was the day Megan told me that her mother had entered the final stages of her emphysema.

As a child, I spent nearly as much time sitting on Megan and Mary's couch as I did at home. My mom and I loved each other, but we fought terribly, both of us strong-willed and stubborn. Once, after a particularly draining fight, I ran to Megan's house. Mary was the one who comforted me. She saw my red-rimmed eyes and, without saying a word, handed me her Nintendo so we could play Tetris. In an hour we were laughing, and I had forgotten what had seemed so important before.

Once at Indian Creek, I dreamed of Mary. Across the river, the land was scorched black. Scarred, whitish trees rose out of the ground like skeletal fingers pointing accusingly at God. In my dream I was looking across the river at the dead trees. Some of them were still burning, but just slightly. Mary was standing in the middle of the charred landscape, and I was crying for her to get away from the fire. But the river ran too fast for her to cross.

Soon after I found out about Mary, my own mother was in Texas, holding on to her brother, who was dying of cancer. Except she probably wasn't holding him. We didn't show love in that way.

I hadn't known my uncle, or any of my extended family. Not well, anyway. My mother's parents had both died by the time she was eleven. My father's father died when I was four. We lived in Idaho, and the rest of the family stretched across Texas, Nevada, Arizona, and Kansas. I had cousins I had never met.

When my uncle was diagnosed, he and my aunt drove across the country in their RV to see us. In his eyes and my mother's eyes, I saw love, but also regret for all those years spent apart. We were all so alone.

THAT HOT, DRY summer was the summer that Caleb and I moved into my parents' basement with baby Reed, and I saw a gentleness in them that I had never noticed before. My mother held Reed so tenderly. I wondered if she had held me that way when I was a baby, and I realized that she probably had.

I wanted to walk Reed over to Megan's house and show him to her mother, but Mary was gone by then.

Because of Mary's role as my childhood confidante, her relationship with my mother had always been strained. I think that my mother was jealous of my affection for Mary, and Mary thought that my mother was too hard on me. Still, in Mary's final moments, my mother—the nurse—spent hours caring for her at her home. It was a generosity, and a redemption of sorts, and I was beginning to realize that no one is ever fully bound by their history.

THAT HOT, DRY summer was the summer I realized that my parents thought Caleb was too good for me. He would wake up first in the mornings and bring Reed to me, then make my lunch for work. One evening, as I was chopping vegetables for a salad, my mother spoke up. "Kelly, your dad and I have been talking, and we think that Caleb does too much for you."

The blade of the knife slid through a tomato. My hand stopped. Red juice leaked on to the cutting board. "What?" I asked.

"He's really generous, but maybe you should step up and do more."

I didn't know how to respond. If he was doing so much, then why was I so tired? Why did I feel so overwhelmed?

I snapped at my mother, "You don't see everything that I do, and you only see how he is at your house. You don't see him at our home. Or his parents' house." It was true. At Caleb's parents' house, I was relegated to the kitchen while he sat on the back porch and drank beer with his father.

My father stepped in and put his hand on my mother's arm. "Honey," he said to my mother, "this is none of our business."

She threw up her arms. "I'm just trying to help," she said.

"He's right; it's not any of your business." I threw down the knife and ran down the stairs to the bedroom that I shared with Caleb.

"What's wrong?" Caleb asked. I started crying, my shoulders shaking. Caleb gathered me into his arms. "I'm so sorry. It doesn't matter what she says. You have me now. I'll always be here for you."

That hot, dry summer was when Caleb told me that if he saw a dirty knife in the sink, he would quickly wash it because he knew that I was the person my mother was going to yell at about it, no matter what.

That hot, dry summer was the first time that a family member—Caleb—acknowledged the ways in which my mother singled me out.

That hot, dry summer was the summer when Caleb began to feel like my real family—all that I had, the entirety of my existence—and I began to feel that, without him, I would be alone.

ONE EVENING DURING my Indian Creek summer, I was sitting on the porch of my cabin alone when I heard branches crack. Quickly. Urgently. I leaned forward, peering around the cabin just in time to see a deer burst out of the pine trees. Her haunches quivered. Hooves spinning. Nostrils flared. Her legs scattered the pine needles, kicking up the soil, unsettling the earth around her. A butterfly darted off in a flutter. My hand rose to my mouth involuntarily, my gut wrenching sideways.

Something was chasing her. I knew this. I moved back closer to the door, still angling my head to watch. The doe disappeared into another thicket of trees, and then the hunter appeared: a wolf, gray and lanky. His face pushed forward, eyes concentrated, the fur on his shoulders spiking, but I could see he wasn't running as fast as he could. He was pacing himself—trotting.

I stepped off the porch and looked up the hillside. He took no notice of me. I scrutinized the trees above the cabin for anything—shadows, maybe, evidence of a pack—but I saw only pine trees with blue skies peeking through the boughs. Still, I knew that wolf probably wasn't alone. He wasn't running fast enough. When he disappeared into the trees, I shut myself in the cabin and sat down at the desk to read a three-year-old magazine left by a former ranger, someone else familiar with boredom and isolation.

Later, I went for a trail run alongside the river. This was the wilderness Abbey had written about; every noise was magnified. The sound of the water combined with the sound of the wind, and the tree branches swayed and rustled. I stopped when I saw some scat on the trail, kneeled down, grabbed a stick, and poked at it. It was wolf scat. Fresh. I stood up suddenly, breathing fast from my jog, and looked around. I had the eerie feeling of being watched. The hair on the back of my neck rose, but I shook off the feeling and continued. I wanted to run to Pungo.

Pungo, an archaeological site just below Indian Creek, was full of pit houses—ancient dugouts that the Shoshone Indians had lived in or used for storage. All that remained of the pit houses were indentations in the ground—barely recognizable—like potholes, but once in Pungo, my imagination always took over. I'd wonder what the wilderness had looked like all of those years ago, whether the magic would have been more accessible to me then.

I turned a corner, almost there, and stopped. Just to the side of the trail, I saw a hooved leg. I stepped closer. It was the deer. She had been torn apart—not inefficiently— legs pulled off and stomach wide open. Blood stained the ground above and below her, but there were no guts or innards around; she had been picked clean. Except for her eye. One eye—glossy and white—stared at me from her skull. It looked at me accusingly. Or pleadingly.

I wanted to cry out, *I couldn't help you*. I almost said it out loud.

THAT HOT, DRY summer was the summer when I found out that Caleb had cheated on me while we were dating. Our relationship had been so short before we married that it had happened early on, but the infidelity still stung. I found out about the cheating because I had a hunch, and I pushed, and he finally told me.

It was a woman he had gone to high school with.

And another woman from the bar where I met him.

And yet another woman—a sex worker in a Nevada brothel.

Years later, when I was still pushing for an explanation, and there was no answer that would satisfy me, he exploded and said about the woman he had gone to high school with, "She treated me like shit in high school, and I wanted to fuck her."

He said about the woman from the bar, "I don't know why I did it. She was fat."

He said about the sex worker, "I wanted to be able to do whatever I wanted to her. I wanted to feel powerful."

But he said none of those things during that hot, dry summer. Not that it would have made a difference.

THAT HOT, DRY summer was when I thought, I have married a man I do not know at all. That hot, dry summer was when I told my coworker Ben about Caleb's cheating, and Ben told me about his father, who had cheated on his mother. "My dad is also a real asshole," he said. "He's pretty abusive. We fought this weekend, and when I tried to drive away, my dad jumped on top of the car." I thought, Caleb sounds exactly like Ben's dad.

THAT HOT, DRY summer was when I kicked Caleb out of my parents' basement and made him stay in a hotel—when my parents tried to talk me out of being so angry—when I went to the hotel, so that Caleb and I could talk—when in Caleb's room, I put Reed on the ground and then sank to the hard floor and wept beside my baby—when I told Caleb that I didn't want to be married to him anymore—when he begged me to change my mind—when I stood up to leave, and he went into a rage.

He pinned me against the wall, and I remembered that chair hitting the wall above our bed. "Let me go," I begged. Reed wailed and held up his arms. "Let me go!" I shouted. "Reed is crying." Caleb unpinned me, and I grabbed Reed, then ran out of the hotel room, down a long, dark hallway, and into the parking lot, where I stopped and blinked at the sudden sunshine.

Heat bore down on me. Reed's thumb was in his mouth, his head on my shoulder, his weight heavy in my arms. I didn't know what to do.

I went home and said nothing to my parents. "Marriage is hard," my mom said when she saw my red eyes, not un-kindly. "It is so hard sometimes."

SOLITUDE IS OVERRATED. "Somewhere in the depths of solitude," wrote Edward Abbey, "beyond wilderness and freedom, lay the trap of madness." At Indian Creek, I re-membered, the solitude wore on me. I hadn't found the in-ner fulfillment that I was looking for, so I was relieved when my coworker Rick arrived. Shortly after his arrival, the trees shook forebodingly. The wind picked up quickly, and raindrops blew sideways into me. Rick was standing on the stoop. "We should head into a cabin," I said.

Rick looked at me and shook his head. "The cabins are surrounded by trees that could fall. The thinning crew identified them as hazard trees. We'd better find a low spot somewhere. Come on. Let's head to that rock." He grabbed my hand just as thunder cracked right next to us. I jumped. The wind was furious now. "Hurry!" he yelled over the wind. We ran and crouched on a large, flat rock perched on the edge of the river canyon just as the downpour started.

I was terrified, but Rick was laughing. "I love storms!" he shouted. He looked at me intensely. "Breathe," he said.

"What?" I asked.

"Like this," he said, taking a deep, long breath through his nose into his chest. "When storms come up like this, the air is charged with negative ions, and they'll make you feel joy. No one really knows why, but the same thing happens when you walk under a waterfall. The negative ions in the air by waterfalls, and oceans, and in storms will make you happy. They release endorphins."

I was skeptical. He looked at my confused face and smiled. "You think I'm crazy!" he shouted. "But I'm right."

He took another long, deep breath and laughed. He really did look crazy, with his long beard and broad smile. I started to laugh too. He crouched on that rock and beat his fists into his chest, shouting madly. He smiled at me, took my hand, and I took a deep breath.

I felt something expanding inside my chest—fear, excitement, happiness—it was unclear what it was. Lightning boomed above me, and I looked up just in time to see a tree sway and then crash into the ground. A great plume of ash rose like smoke. Then another tree fell, and another. The world was shaking, rumbling, and cracking, and I was perched on a rock in the middle of it, holding hands with a strange man.

I had come to the wilderness seeking change through solitude, and I hadn't found it because I wasn't ready. The woods couldn't heal me when all I could think about was Megan, Mary, my mom—people I loved who were hurting while I was unable to help. But when the storm ended, I felt released. Maybe Rick's crazy ideas about negative ions had worked, but I don't think it was that. For a moment, my loneliness had abated. I felt connected to—touched by— another person.

THAT HOT, DRY summer, three years later, I went away for a few days to do some stream sampling with Ben and one other young man. We stayed in a cabin together near a ghost town, but Ben and the other man bought beer and escaped to a nearby hot spring. I sat on the porch of that cabin and thought of my cabin at Indian Creek. It was all so beautiful, but what was the purpose in the beauty if I had no one to share it with? Now I missed my baby, and I missed my husband. This was not the time to reinvent myself.

I went home and told Caleb that we could remain married, but things needed to change. We would need to get couples counseling. He would have to work on his temper, and he would have to earn back my trust. He wrapped me in his arms and broke down into sobs. "I'm so sorry," he said. "I'm so, so sorry. I will fix this. I will make things better." I felt my shoulders softening into his embrace, but still, there was a new hardness inside me.

"Thank you so much for loving me enough to give me another chance," he said, as he held my face in his hands and kissed me.

"Everyone deserves a second chance," I said.

THAT HOT, DRY summer, I spent my days looking at rocks, feeling them in my hands, measuring them, and I learned to find their beauty within. One day I found a rock that glowed silver and green, and I turned it into a totem. When I worried about my marriage, I held that weight in my hand. I told myself that everything would be okay—that as long as I was married, I would never be alone.

10

Take Me to the River

WHEN THE SCHOOL year began, we moved back to Boise. An older friend of mine who had worked with me in the forest service was renting us a house for an amount that we could afford. It was a clean little house on a tidy street in an orderly neighborhood with a large fenced yard and a garden. It was the kind of house where a family could be happy.

IN AUGUST, JUST before we moved back to Boise, Caleb and I left Reed with my parents for a couple of days and drove to Boise to make arrangements for the move. We stayed in a hotel and went to see my therapist. We talked about Caleb's betrayal, about my feelings of resentment, and about how to move forward. We did not talk about Caleb's anger. We talked about what *I* could do differently. The answer was clear: I had to be more forgiving, more tolerant, and more accepting of Caleb's flaws. I was too hard, he said.

I felt this hardness inside me; I knew it to be true.

THE THERAPIST ASKED Caleb why he hadn't told me the truth. "Because she would have punished me," he said. The word *punish* continued to recur from him, and I was baffled. What did he mean by *punish*?

Finally the therapist said to Caleb, "Did your mother punish you when she was angry?"

"Yes," he said. "If I skipped church on a Sunday evening, she would have still been giving me the silent treatment on Tuesday."

The therapist then asked, "Do you think that Kelly punishes you?"

He thought for a long time and then said, "No, I guess not."

It was true. I rarely held grudges. My own mother had been short-tempered, but she was not a grudge holder. She never held things against me for very long, and my father was almost oddly calm. Punishing was not behavior that I had seen modeled at home, but although I didn't have the extremes of my mother's temper, I did have a temper.

I had spent my twenties in therapy, trying to learn how to forgive. I wanted to forgive my mother for how hard she was on me, and I wanted to forgive myself for how hard I was on her in return. I hadn't wanted to have children because I was afraid that I would duplicate the dynamic I'd had with my mother in my own family, but it never occurred to me that I would marry an angry person rather than becoming one. Therapy taught me how to accept accountability for my insecurities and my failings, but maybe I grew too willing to accept accountability. I was more inclined to blame myself when I was angry than I was to blame Caleb.

After that therapy session, we went back to our hotel, and I held Caleb tenderly, said that I was sorry. I felt a kinship with the broken boy inside him who had craved his mother's approval, and I wanted to love that boy the way he had never been loved. We went for a swim in the hotel pool. I had sobbed at the therapist's office, and then again in the hotel, and my eyes were puffy and red. My body felt so heavy, but in that cool, blue water, Caleb picked me up and wrapped my legs around his waist. He held me, and the heaviness lifted.

STILL, THE NEXT day, on the six-hour drive home to my parents' house, we argued. About something. Anything. Soon we were screaming. I felt that I was drowning. No matter what I said, it was turned against me. I wanted to make it stop. I almost wanted to jump out of the moving car, but then Caleb stopped in the middle of the highway. He got out of the driver's side, ran across the road, and threw the keys off the hillside. I got out, too, and just stood there. He had thrown the keys onto a rock field, where they fell in a crevice between the rocks that was dark and endless. The keys were gone. I looked at the car—both doors open—in the middle of the highway. We were on a deserted stretch of highway, and we didn't have a spare key with us.

The Salmon River, dark and fast, rushed below us.

I REMEMBERED THE last time that we had stared at the river together. A few weeks earlier, just after I decided to stay with Caleb, our little family had gone to Dagger Falls, where the salmon jump. They are called Dagger Falls because of the sharp black rocks that poke out of the frothy white water. As I stared at the falls, Reed in my arms and Caleb beside me, I thought back to the summer when I worked at Indian Creek. I had found an arrowhead at Dagger Falls, black obsidian carved into a sharp point, and I had pocketed it, even though I shouldn't have. *Take only memories. Leave only footprints.* I had tried to take a part of that wilderness home with me, but I lost my treasure somewhere along the way. Maybe it was karma. Maybe I lost the arrowhead because I never should have tried to take something that didn't belong to me. Maybe I didn't deserve to have anything beautiful in my life.

The salmon sprang out of the water. They hit the rocks with loud thwacks. It must have been painful. Some of them found the right route—natural steps built into the falls that they could navigate—but some of them did not. One of them kept flopping back into the water, shocked for a moment, then sprang back up and jumped again. Hit the black rock again. Fell again. And again. And again. It couldn't change its nature.

"Isn't it beautiful?" I asked Caleb. "The persistence?"

"But aren't they just returning to the place of their birth so they can die?"

I stared at that fish, fighting for its right to die. "I guess so," I said. I thought of Greg and the fish biologist, of how much it had hurt when those lovers left me, of how I hadn't let go of that hurt until I met Caleb. I thought of how I'd hoped that when we married, it meant I would never have to hurt like that again. I looked at Caleb and felt that we wouldn't be married forever.

I held Reed in my arms. He smiled at me and reached his

little hands out to touch my face. The water raged below us, and for a moment, I wanted to jump.

I smiled at Reed, holding him up above the water, so that he, too, could see the salmon jumping, their silver and red bodies glinting like blades. Reed laughed. I held him tight. I couldn't jump. I couldn't let him be swept into those waves with me.

THOSE WEEKS LATER, as I stood there in the middle of the highway—alone with Caleb—the thought flashed into my head again: *I could jump.* Caleb scrambled down the rocky hillside. He snatched up the keys as if he had known all along that he was going to find them. He came back to the car. "Look what you made me do," he said.

I was so tired, I had no more energy for fighting; I barely had enough energy to survive. I got back into the passenger seat, pressed my head to the window, and stared out the glass at the dry mountains of the river canyon rushing past me. My anger was gone. I felt only relief. It was the same lightening of my body that I had felt when Caleb gripped my legs and held me in that blue swimming pool. The feeling was oddly sweet. In some strange way, I even felt tender toward Caleb, as though the only person who could ever understand the flash of panic I felt when he threw those keys over the hillside was him. As though we were in it together.

And after all, maybe it *had* been my fault. I had been angry. Maybe he did the only thing that he could to stop my anger; he replaced it with fear.

WHEN WE MOVED into the little house in Boise, we were in a different part of town from our friends, and I grew lonely. I rode my bike through residential neighborhoods to a nearby river trail where I continued the three miles to campus. That bike ride along the calm Boise River was the highlight of my days. While I was on that bike, I felt a freedom that I didn't feel at home. The heaviness lifted, and sunlight glittered on the water.

By then, the heaviness had become a part of my body. Even sunlight felt heavy. Reed continued to be a joy, but beyond that, I felt so little. As the summer turned to autumn, the sunlight grew heavier and heavier. I could feel its weight on my skin. I did everything that I could to find more energy. I knew that exercise was important, so I would put Reed in the jogging stroller and jog or walk around our neighborhood. I always asked if Caleb wanted to go with me, and he almost always said no. The distance between us was growing, and I was lonelier in that marriage than I had ever been before. Sometimes I cried when he said no, and he would yell at me, "Quit crying. You want me to do everything with you. You don't respect my writing time."

Sometimes I would lie in bed and cry for no reason at all, and he would stand in the door and scream at me, "Quit crying. What are you crying about?" I would only cry more, then, and say, "I don't know why I'm crying. I just don't know."

By then we were arguing more, and I was beginning to feel afraid of him. He would back me into corners while he yelled at me, and I felt so helpless. Once he pushed me against the wall and pinned me. I panicked, lashing out and hitting him in the face. The wire on his glasses broke, and the lens fell out. He pulled back, the lens in his hand, and I stared in horror. What had I done?

I begged him to forgive me, and he did, scooping me into his arms and telling me that it was okay, that he understood. I was so grateful for his forgiveness. He taped his lens back into his glasses, then offered to go for a walk with me. We walked the stroller to the river and took Reed out. Reed toddled to the banks and threw rocks into the water, while Caleb held on to the back of his shirt to keep him from jumping in. As I watched the way that Caleb protected Reed, again, the heaviness lifted, replaced with tenderness. Caleb held my hand on the way home, and when we got home, he put Reed to bed, made me dinner, and then tucked my head into his chest. The loneliness abated. Neither of us was perfect, but we shared an intimacy. We were all that we had.

OCTOBER CAME, AND the light continued to have this quality of intensity and dimness at the same time. I was no longer trying to be happy; I was only trying to be not-depressed. I took Reed for long walks, and felt myself teetering on a razor's edge. On one side of that edge was beauty, and on the other side of that edge was despair.

As Reed and I walked alongside the river, I could see into the yards of fancy homes. I wondered what their families were like. Did they, too, feel that something was missing? I finally went to the student health center and told the doctor that I had been feeling depressed. She gave me a depression screening, and after I finished answering the questions, she left the room and then came back. "We cannot let you go on like this," she said. "Do you think about suicide?"

"Yes," I answered, "but I would never do it. I only fantasize about it."

"How often do you fantasize about it?" she asked.

"Every day," I said.

I left her office with a prescription for Prozac. I wasn't particularly interested in saving myself, but I hoped that I had finally found the way to save my marriage.

I CONTINUED TO see my therapist and continued to tell her about how unhappy I was in my marriage. The Prozac had only achieved a manageable state of numbness for me. I wanted her to teach me how to be happy. Occasionally I would bring Caleb in to see her with me, and he would always talk about how critical I was of him, and how frustrated he felt living with me. After one session she gave us an activity: we were to take a week off from criticism. No matter what, we could not criticize each other. The first couple of days were wonderful. I enjoyed not criticizing him. I enjoyed letting things slide.

Soon, though, he was criticizing me. "That's criticism," I would say. "Oh wow, you're right," he would say, and then we would both laugh. It had become a game for us, but at the end of the week, we both realized that I was not the one in the marriage who was prone to criticism. We went back in to my therapist's office and sat side by side on the couch. "What did you realize this week?" she asked.

Caleb didn't pause. "I realized that I am actually very critical of Kelly," he said, "and that I am too hard on her." I was so proud of him for being honest with her. I reached over and squeezed his hand.

She seemed surprised. "Wow," she said. "I hadn't expected that. How did that make you feel, Kelly?"

I paused, and then said, "I was surprised, too, but I feel better now. I think that we're better now."

Caleb and I went home that day and congratulated ourselves. We had done what needed to be done. We had gotten therapy. I had started taking medication. We were working on not arguing so much. We were going to be okay. I knew it.

THE FOLLOWING WEEK, we fought again, and again I went to see my therapist. She was obviously disappointed to hear that we were still struggling. "When things get that tense," she said, "you need to go somewhere. You need to exit the situation."

"But I can't," I said. "He won't let me."

"What do you mean, he won't let you?"

"I mean, he will get in front of me, or back me into the corner. Once he even held me to the wall. I panicked and hit him in the face, so that he would let me leave."

She sat back, her face concerned. "Kelly, that is domestic violence. What he is doing to you is domestic violence."

I was confused. "But he has never hit me," I said. "I'm the one who hit him."

"Yes," she said, "but hitting someone to escape is not the same thing as hitting someone to control them, and when he is pinning you to the wall or backing you into a corner, then that is physical intimidation, and that is a method of control. It is part of a pattern of violence." She reached into her filing cabinet. "I am going to give you this flyer," she said. "It is for the domestic violence shelter, and I want you to keep it for if you need it." She pulled out a purple paper and handed it to me.

I stared at the paper. I had no idea what to think. I knew that I wasn't being abused. He had never hit me, and I was strong. I was independent. I was the girl who had run away from Danny, and who had escaped that man in the truck. I was not someone who would be abused.

I tucked the paper into my bag and then rode my bike home. I decided to tell Caleb what the therapist had said. I didn't think that he was abusing me, but I did want him to stop intimidating me. I knew that when he heard that my therapist thought he was abusing me, he would realize what he had been doing. His honesty about the criticism had shown me that he was willing to be self-reflective. This was only going to improve things.

At home, he asked me how it went, and I motioned for him to sit next to me on the couch. I pulled out the flyer. "She thinks that you are being abusive," I said, then waited for him to respond with compassion.

He flew into a rage. "Are you saying that I'm a domestic abuser?" he yelled. "Are you kidding me?"

I shrank. "No, I'm not saying that," I said. "She's saying that. I just thought that it might make you realize that what you've been doing is wrong." I put my hand on his arm.

"Fuck that," he said, shaking my hand off. "This is bullshit. I do everything for you, and you don't even appreciate it."

"No, I do," I said. "I do appreciate all that you do for me."

"Then why don't you respect me? Why would you believe someone who says such awful things about me?"

I was drowning again—in the same way that I had been drowning in the car. There was no way out, nothing I could say that would make him believe me, and I no longer even knew if I was right. Maybe he was right. Maybe I was wrong, and my therapist was wrong, and the real problem was my lack of respect for him.

The water closed over my head. I couldn't breathe. I gave in. "You're right," I said. "Of course you're right. I'm sorry."

THE NEXT DAY I took Reed for our walk, and we walked by an irrigation ditch instead of the river. The ditch was deep, the water so swift. A fence surrounded the water, marked with "Danger" and "Keep Away" signs. I knew that people had drowned in that ditch, but there was still an attraction to the water, a beauty in its swiftness.

Reed and I walked above our neighborhood and stopped at one particular home, my breath gathering in my chest. In the middle of striped green grass was a swimming pool—

blue and clean and clear—surrounded by reclining chairs on a patio. I wanted so badly to live in that home, to dip myself into the clean depths of that pool, to fill those chairs with Reed, and with Caleb, and with the other children that we might have. There would be so much love there. I would find a way to create that home. I wasn't ready to give up on that hope yet.

11

Broken Things

THE FIRST THING I broke was an orange Fiestaware plate. I was in the kitchen, taking the dishes out of the dishwasher, and Caleb was angry about something. I attempted to ignore him but he loomed over me and pushed my back up to the sink, his anger trapping me. When I tried to move around him, he moved with me. A frustration like I had never felt before rose in me. Without any consciousness of what I was doing, I threw the plate I was holding to the ground with such force that it shattered.

Caleb and I both looked at the broken plate—a cheerful orange—on the beige linoleum. His face was smug. *Now look what you've done*, it said.

I stared at the shattered ceramic. What was wrong with me?

I got out the broom and swept the shards into the dustpan. I had no idea then that sweeping up broken things would become the new normal.

AT THAT TIME, Megan was in graduate school in Moscow, Idaho, and engaged to be married. Because Megan's mother had died, her mother's friends—including my mother— threw her a bridal shower. They decided to host it in Boise, which was where most of Megan's friends lived, and I was looking forward to an escape from my loneliness.

MEGAN HAD BEEN the maid of honor in my wedding, and had hosted a "Silly Dress" party at my bridal shower. I wore a dress festooned with pictures of playing cards. Megan wore a dress with flowers and a large collar that looked like something the Mormon churchgoers would have worn when we were kids. Everyone was joyful, and at that party, surrounded by my friends, I first met Joanne and my sister-in-law, and Caleb's grandmother and his aunt. I was four months pregnant and had slept in the car the night before, so despite the festiveness of the event, my eyes were dark circles.

THE DAY BEFORE, my mother and I had driven six hours round-trip over a 7,000-foot mountain pass on the Continental Divide to buy supplies at the Costco in Missoula for the wedding. It was a long day of shopping, and on our drive home the car suddenly made a loud scraping noise and shuddered to a stop. We were still about twenty miles from town. We got out of the car and walked alongside the river to the nearest farmhouse, where we banged on the doors. "I know them from the hospital," Mom said. "They are old and not going to hear us."

We turned around and walked back to the car. We both knew that there weren't homes for at least a mile or two down the road, but what were we supposed to do? We started walking, headed toward a dark section of the river canyon called

Red Rock where, when I was in high school, students would jump off a huge red boulder into deep water. It was the place where I had taken swigs of cheap Idaho Silver vodka in a car with two boys and my best friend. While she made out with one of the boys in the front seat, I sat uncomfortably in the back seat with the other. At that time, I was always the girl in the back seat the boys didn't want to make out with.

MY MOTHER AND I entered the dark canyon. The cottonwood trees loomed above us, and no moon peeked through the trembling leaves. Suddenly a wolf howled, and then another, and soon the howls of the wolves ricocheted off the river walls. My mother stopped. She put her hand on my arm. I was unsteady, but she was firm. "Let's turn around," she said, guiding me, and walked briskly back the other way. I let myself be pulled along beside her. My mother was strong. She always knew what to do. We slept in the car until a vehicle drove by at 6:00 a.m., and a woman who knew us gave us a ride. My father went to retrieve the car and took it to a mechanic, but the mechanic never found anything wrong with it.

AT MY BRIDAL shower, I set my fatigue aside and greeted my new family. I liked all of them immediately, except Joanne. There was a frozen look on her face. Perhaps she was as scared as I was, but I already felt that I would never win her approval. Later everyone sat in a circle and told stories about me. My first boss, Karen, told of how I had gone into her bookstore when I was only fifteen and said that I thought she should employ me because I read a book a day. She described me as being spunky and smart, and said that she had always thought of me as a little sister. My friend Sadie told how I used to play the kazoo as a party trick. She described me as being one of the funniest people she knew. Sadie looked directly at Joanne and said, "Kelly is really special. You are so lucky to have her joining your family." I had never felt more loved.

After the party, my new grandmother-in-law hugged me. She said, "It was so wonderful to hear the stories about you. You are going to be so good for Caleb. You will find that our family has secrets. We have skeletons in our closet, but you will be good for him."

Caleb's best female friend from West Virginia, who had also attended the shower, said, "You are perfect. Caleb needs someone like you."

It seemed to be a theme—*Caleb needs someone like you.*

I didn't question it. I liked being needed. It never occurred to me to ask myself if I needed someone like Caleb.

LATER, WHEN I asked Caleb about those skeletons, he said, "She had a stroke. She has never been the same. She doesn't know what she's talking about."

I PLANNED THE wedding within three months, and everything about it felt rushed. Caleb and I had only known each other for eight months. The night before my wedding, when my father was sleeping and I was alone in the kitchen, I broke into sobs. My mother came in and hugged me for the first time in a long time. She looked at me and said, "Listen to me. It is never too late. You don't have to do this."

"Yes, I do," I said.

Just then, Kelly M. and another friend burst in through the door. They had been out at the Owl Club with Caleb and his friends and family. While I had been crying in the kitchen with my mother, Caleb had been singing a song he wrote called "The Porta-John Song," while his friends laughed and cheered him on. He was so funny, but no matter how many times I asked, he would never sing that song to me—not through eight years of marriage. There was a lot about Caleb that he would never let me see.

Kelly M. saw my puffy face, my tears. "Oh, hon," she said, putting her arm around my shoulder and leading me to my bedroom. "Let's go to bed."

THE NEXT DAY, at the wedding reception, Megan gave her maid-of-honor speech. She told her own story this time. She described how, when we were little girls, I would often charge into the street without watching for cars. She described how she always had to reach out and pull me back.

She looked at Caleb, and her voice cracked. "That's your job now," she said. "Don't let her rush into incoming traffic without looking both ways. It's your job to keep her safe."

THE DAY OF Megan's own bridal shower, I spent the morning cleaning the house in a rush. Megan hadn't seen Reed since he was a newborn, and she was going to come over and visit before we went to the shower together. I was excited to show her our house, and to show off Reed, who by then was a darling ten-month-old. As I cleaned, Caleb's mood grew dark. "Why do you need to clean so much?" he asked. "It's just Megan. She doesn't care how the house looks."

"I just want it to look nice," I said. He was grumpy, but I knew that he would get over it when Megan arrived. He was always cheerful when other people were around.

Just as Megan was due to arrive, I received a phone call from her. She was stuck downtown with a different friend. "It's okay," I said. "That's fine. No worries." Still, I hung up the phone and started crying. I wasn't angry at her, but I was disappointed, and I had always been an easy crier.

Caleb hated my easy tears, and this was no exception. He screamed, "Why are you crying? This is not about you. This is about Megan. You are making this about you."

His rage overwhelmed me, and I started to sob. I couldn't articulate what I was feeling, which was that I was disappointed, hurt, and a little bit jealous of that other friend, but that it was really no big deal, and I would be over my hurt feelings in time for the shower. The weight of Caleb's fury kept me from saying any of that. All I could do was sob.

He screamed, a loud, guttural scream, and I shrank back, shaking. His scream worked. My sobs stopped. He picked up Reed's baby bouncer and threw it against the wall. Reed was sleeping in his crib. The bouncer was his favorite toy. I stared. Shivers seemed to come all the way from my organs.

I started to hiccup. I couldn't talk. "You're being hysterical," Caleb screamed at me.

He pointed at the clock. It was almost time for the shower. "I can't drive like this," I gasped, between hiccups.

"Get ready, and I'll drive you," he yelled. "God, I have to do everything for you."

I went into the bathroom and saw my face. I was an ugly crier. The tears came back. I went outside. "I'm not going," I said.

By then, Caleb had calmed down.

I called Megan. I didn't know what to say, so I told her that Caleb and I had a fight, and I wasn't in a state to attend the party. Her voice was worried. "Are you okay?" she asked.

"I'm okay," I said, as fast as I could because I wanted off the phone before I broke into tears again. "I'm sorry."

"It's okay," she said. "I'll tell your mom."

AFTER I HUNG up the phone, I watched Caleb put the pieces of Reed's bouncer in the trash outside. I looked over and saw the neighbor woman, an older Mormon woman, looking at us out of her window. Her eyes were compassionate.

Caleb came back in the house. "I'm sorry," he said. "I shouldn't have broken Reed's baby bouncer."

"I just needed you to listen," I said. "Then I would have been fine, but you scared me."

"I know, and there's no excuse for that. I acted horribly," he said. "I don't know what came over me. I should have just listened to you. Of course your feelings would be hurt that your friend broke your plans, and you went to so much effort to get the house looking nice. I know that you would have been fine for the shower. I really messed up. Can you forgive me?"

I was no longer afraid, and his compassion felt so sweet, so needed. "You're such a good friend," he said. "And such a good wife and mother. I don't deserve you."

"Of course you do," I said. And I meant it. Of course he deserved me. Or maybe I deserved him. Maybe we just deserved each other.

THAT NIGHT MY mother came over, and she didn't ask any questions. She told us to go out to dinner, to have a night off, that she would watch Reed. Caleb and I ate at our favorite restaurant. We laughed and had a good time, but my feelings were still tender. Caleb drank three beers with dinner, and in the car on the way home, I said something about being upset that I had missed Megan's shower. "Why won't you ever let anything go?" he yelled. "I thought that we had put this behind us." I couldn't believe that he was yelling again. It made me feel like his apology had meant nothing.

When we got home, I marched into the house, past my mother, and went to the fridge. I took out Caleb's beer and went into the backyard. I dropped the bottles one by one onto the cement patio. They shattered, and then I went back into the house. I looked at Caleb and my mother. "I'm done," I said. "I can't do this anymore."

My mother sent Caleb to our bedroom. She took me into

the backyard, and I told her, "He's so mean to me, Mom. He loses his temper, and I'm scared of him. He lies to me, and I don't trust him. I've never been more miserable."

I wanted my mother to tell me that she would fix it. I wanted her to fix it in the way that she had fixed everything before, but she couldn't fix this. She looked at me straight on and said, "Listen to me. It is not better on the other side. I have seen it on the other side. Try hard. Try hard before you give up."

I stared through the glass door into the house. I knew that my baby was sleeping in there. I knew that I couldn't afford that house on my own. I thought of my mother's friends, the ones who had left their husbands, who had lived on "the other side." I thought of the ways they had lapsed into poverty, or worse, into relationships that were uglier than the ones they had left.

I knew that Caleb loved Reed and me, that he felt remorse, and at that time, I thought I wasn't the greatest catch myself. Hadn't I been breaking things too? Hadn't I gotten hysterical at a slight disappointment by my best friend? I had never felt more inadequate in my life, less worthy of love.

My mother hugged me. "Go to bed," she said. "I will clean this up." I went to bed, crawled in next to Caleb, and he pulled me into his arms. Even when I was angry, I loved the way that my body fit into his. I loved the way he always held me so freely.

Even when he was angry at me, with his back turned, he would still let me wrap my body around his. Always, I could feel the way that he would soften into my embrace. He could never stay angry for too long, and neither could I. We fit each other too well to stay angry.

The next morning, when I woke up, my mother was gone.

A COUPLE OF days later, there was a knock at the door. Two young male Mormon missionaries stood on the stoop. In high school, I had sometimes hung out with the Mormon missionaries for fun, but I had never received an impromptu visit. I gave them the line that I had always heard my mother use with Jehovah's Witnesses: "I already have a religion."

One of them spoke up. "We just thought there might be someone here who wanted to talk," he said.

"No, I'm fine, thanks."

The other one piped up, "There's no one here who wants to talk? Maybe a young mother in distress with a child?"

I looked back at Reed playing on the floor and understood. The neighbor had called them. I looked back at the missionaries in their black slacks and white shirts.

I hesitated, and then said, "No, there is no young mother in distress here."

As they walked away, I briefly thought about running after them, but I closed the door instead.

I just needed to try harder.

12

Playlist for a Broken Heart

I KNEW THAT SOMETHING needed to change, but I wasn't sure what that something was. We didn't have much money. I was still in college, and Caleb was teaching five classes as an adjunct instructor at Boise State University. When we couldn't pay the bills, Caleb would gather up our books and CDs, take them to the Hastings on the corner, and sell them. My heart hurt as Caleb walked out the door, a paper bag full of books in his arms. Fortunately, Reed was covered by the Children's Health Insurance Program, and because my friend had rented her house to us for only $550 a month, we were able to scrape by on what we had.

After the day of Megan's shower, Caleb hovered anxiously around me, always reaching out to touch me for reassurance. If I ate a sandwich, he would have the dirty plate out of my hands before I could stand up. He went for long walks with me and cooked wonderful meals. He changed Reed's diapers and vacuumed the floor. I was confused by this sudden change, and I felt guilty that he was being so helpful.

Still, he was irritable. If I tried to bring up something that upset me, he would yell, "Look at everything I've done for you! Doesn't that count for something?" Sometimes, he would get angry and scare me so much that I would burst into tears and start shivering. By then the shivering had become normal. I didn't understand what had happened to me—when had I become so weak and hysterical?

Sometimes Caleb would say, "Now you've made me act so awful that I have to apologize to *you*." Confusion and guilt rose in my chest. Had I created his anger? Had I pushed him so hard that he was forced to lash out at me in those ways? Was I somehow responsible for his behavior? I only knew that I no longer felt like myself. I was weepy and irritable. Maybe he was right and I had made him into the person he had become.

I STARTED GOING to Kelly M.'s when we fought. Reed was such a good sleeper by then that he went to bed every night at six and slept until six in the morning, so I knew that I could leave him sleeping peacefully and return before he woke. And the truth was that Caleb was a wonderful father.

Though Caleb was unpredictable with me, he was patient and loving with Reed. I had grown up in a culture where, outside of sports, men didn't participate much in their children's lives, but Caleb wasn't that kind of father. He would wake first in the morning with Reed and let me sleep in. When I would come into the living room, I would find them on the couch together, Reed cuddled up on Caleb's chest or Caleb doing something silly to make Reed squeal with laughter.

Caleb was not a part-time dad. He was as present for Reed as I was.

AT HEART I knew that in some ways, Caleb might be even more present for Reed than I was. Caleb would play games with Reed and make him laugh, but much of the time I was too sad to be playful. I knew that Caleb wasn't struggling with sadness, or distrust, or confusion about whether he had made the right decisions in his life.

I knew that it was hard for me to be fully present for Reed when I was curled up in bed, crying.

KELLY M. WOULD make up a bed for me on the couch, loan me pajamas, and then crawl in next to me. I don't remember much about those evenings. I remember that Kelly M.'s apartment was cold and small, and it didn't feel like a home. I remember that her pajamas didn't fit me right.

YEARS LATER, KELLY M. would tell me that I would talk for hours about what was going on with Caleb, that I would be determined to leave, but then, at some point in the evening, I would fatigue, soften, and suddenly say, "I just want to be with my husband."

She said that I never called him Caleb. I called him "my husband." I was fixated on the idea of marriage as sacred, even though she would talk about her own parents divorcing many years too late. She had seen the kind of pain that an unhappy marriage could create, but she knew that I couldn't hear that yet.

IN THE END I would always get up from Kelly M.'s couch, dress again, and go home to "my husband" and my baby. I'd climb into our warm bed, Caleb would pull me in close, and I would relax into the forgiveness. Forgiveness was so much easier than staying angry. Staying angry meant that I would have had to leave, and I simply wasn't up to that.

STILL, SOMETHING HAD changed. I didn't feel the same way about Caleb, and though I couldn't and wouldn't have articulated that to him, he sensed my withdrawal. Finally he grew desperate. Even though we couldn't really afford it, he said, "You need a girls' weekend away. You deserve it. Why don't you see if Jeannie will go on one with you?" I thought of what he had said. Maybe he was right. Maybe I just needed a vacation. I thought that she could give me some advice, help me know how to move forward.

I was also grateful to have a husband who would cheerfully watch our child while I went away for a weekend. Not many women have husbands like this, I thought. I'm very lucky, I thought.

Why didn't I feel lucky?

I CALLED JEANNIE, and it was decided. We were going for a long weekend to Seattle. I flew in a day earlier than Jeannie, booked a bed in a hostel, dropped off my stuff, then walked to Pike Place Market. I had a cup of chowder and browsed the shops. I had always been independent—I was not afraid of traveling by myself—but the marriage had changed me.

Seattle was beautiful, and the travel felt like an adventure, but I couldn't stop thinking of how much I wished that Caleb was there with me. I also couldn't stop thinking of how much I wished I could leave him.

I wondered how it was possible to hold two such completely incongruent thoughts at the same time. More than that, though, I realized that I had grown dependent on Caleb in ways I had never anticipated. There I was, in Seattle, such a beautiful city, and I was unable to enjoy it because I no longer knew how to be by myself. That night I put my stuff in a locker, then got into my bunk bed in a room full of other people. As I lay in that dark room, I could hear the rhythmic breathing around me, but I had never felt so alone.

I THOUGHT THAT it would be better when Jeannie joined me, and at first, it was. Jeannie had such a large presence and joyful spirit. She always knew how to make me feel better, but when I confided to her that I was miserable with Caleb, she confided to me that she, too, was miserable with Jay. Two women in miserable marriages is not a recipe for a fun weekend away.

JEANNIE AND I ate fish and chips on the wharf and took the ferry to Bainbridge Island, but I missed Caleb. The last night that we were there, I called an old friend from college. We all went to a pub and split a bottle of wine, and then Jeannie and I went back to the hostel. I had booked a private room for us, and once we were alone, she cried on the bed, her body shaking with sobs. I was shocked. I had known Jeannie since we were children, and I don't think I had ever seen her cry.

That night she told me secrets about her life, her marriage—dark secrets that tumbled out of her mouth like rocks, secrets I never repeated, secrets that reminded me of the secrets I was keeping about my own marriage. Her despair was so evident that I wanted to protect her. I reassured her that everything would be okay, and I reassured myself of the same thing, but I didn't believe it.

WHEN CALEB PICKED me up at the airport, I hugged him, but I felt at a remove. I wondered if I would be unhappy for as long as Jeannie had been. I wondered how things could ever possibly get better. I wondered how I could support myself and Reed if I left Caleb.

Caleb seemed disappointed by my lack of enthusiasm when I saw him. "I thought that this weekend would have rejuvenated you," he said.

I confided to him that I was drained and disappointed because, instead of Jeannie reassuring me, I felt like I had seen my own future ahead of me, and it was a future of sadness. He seemed so hurt by my statement that I reached across the car and squeezed his hand. I didn't know what else to do.

WHEN WE ARRIVED home, he sat down next to me on the couch. He was nervous. He pulled out an envelope and gave it to me with a compact disc, a mix CD that he had made for me. I remembered how I had made a mix CD for him when we were dating, and he had listened to it in his truck on repeat. I remembered how Cory had told me that, while he and Caleb were driving in the woods listening to my mix CD, Caleb had said that I was the one—the woman he wanted to marry.

HE HAD WRITTEN a letter to accompany the CD, and the letter was an annotated playlist. He had chosen songs from our time together and described the moments that accompanied those songs as a way of reminding me of how special our connection was.

HE WROTE THAT he had chosen "Harvest Moon" because he met me in autumn, and fall was his favorite season. Someday he wanted to take me home to West Virginia in the fall, he said, so that the most beautiful woman in the world could be in the most beautiful place.

HE CHOSE MY favorite song from high school, Depeche Mode's "Personal Jesus," and wrote that in the midst of all of the hipsters at the Neurolux, he had found me seeping empathy. He questioned how he could have possibly found me there.

HE CHOSE "GOLD to Me" because I had looked like gold to him when we met.

FOR THE SONG "Hey, Good Lookin'," he described the way that he had sat next to me on my couch the first night I took him home. He wrote that when he put his arm around me, those were the words that came to mind. He also wrote that he loved that I sang that song to Reed. I would change his diaper, singing those words, kissing his bare belly when I was finished; and then, because Caleb was never far from me, I would turn and hold Reed between my softness and Caleb's hard chest. His eyes were never hard in those moments, and as his arms wrapped around both of us, I would lean in for a kiss and whisper to Caleb, "Hey, Good Lookin'."

"SIMPLY IRRESISTIBLE" REMINDED him of how he had taken me to bed that first night we met. I had worn a thin red-and-white-striped shirt with spaghetti straps, and though we kissed and touched all night, I didn't take off my shirt. He wrote about the song "Can I Sleep In Your Arms?" and how he had asked me to take my shirt off so he could feel my skin against his.

HE WROTE THAT "God's Gonna Cut You Down" made him think of how, when we were dating, he had loved booze and treated me wrong because of that. He wrote that he had talked to God, and asked to be forgiven. He asked me not to rush my forgiveness, that he had to earn it.

"LAY, LADY, LAY" reminded him of how, when he lived in the shack in the woods, he would watch out the window for me for hours, making sure I didn't miss the turn off Highway 21. He described how we would sleep on his couch beside each other, and he never felt crowded because we fit so perfectly together.

HE WROTE THAT he had played "Windfall" a lot when he was in love with me and couldn't tell me yet. He had listened to this song on his way up the mountain, and it was so happy and carefree that it had made him think of me. He wrote that he hoped, forever, the wind would take my troubles away.

He wrote that he wanted me to have the good life I deserve.

"GLORY BOX" MADE him think of the previous Valentine's Day, when after Reed had gone to sleep, we boiled lobsters, cracked the red claws, sucked the meat out of the shell, and licked the greasy butter off our fingers. Then I danced for him, wearing that spaghetti-strap shirt. I had never felt comfortable before with a man in that way, but as I danced, I felt *like a woman*. Later, my fingers dug into his back as he came inside me, again and again.

HE CHOSE "CONCEIVED" because we had made a baby on Valentine's Day. He wrote, "See note for 'Glory Box.'"

"NEVER TEAR US Apart" reminded him of the time he had drunkenly told me that he wanted me to marry him. I wasn't pregnant yet, and we were just two kids in love. He wrote that he had been so scared because he knew that I was the one, and told me that I should never question his love for me.

I remembered that I had been scared, too, that I had thought things were moving too quickly, but his eyes and his gentleness had reassured me that it was okay.

HE WROTE THAT he wished that he had written "Mystifies Me" for me.

"GIVE A MAN a Home" made him think of how I had given him a home when he didn't deserve it. He knew that I had lost my belief in him, but he wanted to restore it.

HE WROTE THAT he wished he could have gone back to high school and stood outside my window holding a boom box while playing "In Your Eyes," just like I had seen John Cusack do in the movie *Say Anything*. In high school I had dreamed of that kind of grand, romantic gesture, but had never thought that any man would do that for me.

Until Caleb.

AND FINALLY, HE wrote of how the song "Standing in the Doorway" made him think of how he had felt on the night in Salmon when I had made him stay in a hotel. He wrote that he hadn't known if he could fix our marriage, that he didn't blame me for what had happened to us, and he begged me to try to forgive him.

When I finished the letter, I was in tears. He had accepted accountability for his actions, and his sincerity was obvious. He wanted to fix the broken things.

More than that, he had perfectly described the shine of our early relationship, a time that had felt like a beautiful haze.

He looked at me, tears in his eyes, and said, "I mean it," and I prayed that he did. I didn't know if I could handle any more sadness.

WHEN I SPOKE to Jeannie a few days later, she reassured me that her blues had been a lapse, that she was happy in her marriage and life. I wanted to believe her. Everyone said that relationships took work. My own mother had told me to try hard, and I was going to try. I remembered the sparkle of those early days. I was not a quitter, and I didn't want to let go of that shine.

13

His Ghost in Her Bones

THE ROSEBRIAR INN, a former convent, was a bed-and-breakfast perched on the upper end of Astoria, Oregon, a town where the Columbia River meets the Pacific. Known as the Graveyard of the Seas due to the deadly mix of currents caused by the merging of the two bodies, Astoria is a city of shipwrecks.

Caleb and I were vacationing there for our second anniversary. My parents were watching Reed for us, and we were enjoying an actual week's vacation during our spring break. We were doing this for two reasons. The first was that Boise State had found that a certain number of adjunct instructors were teaching too many courses, and they had realized they needed to promote those instructors to special lecturers and were offering them benefits and back pay. Caleb had come into a windfall of about $11,000, but it wasn't set to last. When his contract started over, he would be back to an adjunct's salary of $2,500 per class, with no benefits, and he would never be allowed to teach as many classes.

Which led to the second reason we were on this vacation: Caleb and I had decided to move to West Virginia.

There were many compelling reasons for the move. We

had money for the first time. Caleb's parents had a house that they had bought before the bubble and would sell to us cheaply. Caleb could adjunct anywhere, including WVU, so it wasn't like he was going to be out of work. He wanted to be closer to his family, and finally I had come to the realization that my English degree wasn't practical enough for our financial needs. West Virginia University had a master's program in teaching English as a second language that I had thought might be a good fit. Caleb had convinced me that we could get on our feet in West Virginia, establish ourselves, and then move back west.

"We'll be there for five years max," he said.

THE BIGGEST REASON for the move was that our relationship simply wasn't working. I had tried everything—individual therapy, couples therapy, exercise, antidepressants—and I was still miserable. We fought, then made up, then fought again, and I had never been so exhausted. Caleb never seemed to tire. He could fight for hours.

Always, I eventually broke, apologizing and begging for forgiveness.

STILL, REED WAS such a joy. He had a stuffed toy Tigger from Winnie the Pooh that he carried around, and I would call Reed my own little Tigger because he loved to run, and jump, and would break into laughter that shook his entire body. When I would take him to the grocery store, his big eyes and broad grin charmed everyone he met. At night we would cuddle in bed and read *Brown Bear, Brown Bear, What Do You See?*, and though he couldn't read or speak well yet, he would chatter along with me in imitation, his head on my shoulder, his thumb in his cheek.

He wasn't a cuddly child, was generally too busy for snuggles, but when he was tired, he would hold his arms up to me and say, "Carry me. Carry me."

For years, even when he was nowhere nearby, I would think that I could hear his voice crying, *Carry me. Carry me.*

Once, when Kelly M. was visiting, Reed was crawling in the hallway, and I pounced on him and kissed him all over. "He's just so cute," I said. "I've never been one of those people to make up silly songs for babies, but I can't help myself with him." Caleb adored Reed, too, and something that we always agreed on was that Reed was our greatest happiness.

The money and the move to West Virginia was exciting, and suddenly Caleb and I were getting along. We drove to Portland, Oregon, and laughed the entire way. In Portland we ate good food and went to shops, but mostly, we had sex. We had so much sex that I felt as though my chest had cracked open, and Caleb had crawled inside it. If I could have, I would have let him inside my own skin. I felt as connected to him as I had during the shiny early days of the relationship.

After Portland, we drove up the coast to Astoria, where we landed at the Rosebriar Inn. We went out for a dinner of salmon, then back to our room, where we drank wine, had sex again, and then watched *General Hospital*, my weakness.

When the theme song came on, he danced into the room playing air saxophone, and I laughed, then opened my arms to him so that he could crawl into them and lay his head on my chest. We fell asleep like that.

And then I woke suddenly. It was as though a fist had cracked me on the head. I could feel the pain. I was awake, but I couldn't move. A woman was sitting on my chest. She was afraid. This wasn't the first time I had suffered from sleep paralysis. One night, after a terrible fight with Caleb, I woke, convinced that a large wooden stake had speared me to the bed. Finally I screamed. Caleb grabbed me and held me tightly in his arms.

"You're safe," he said as I trembled into his chest. "You're safe."

THAT NIGHT IN Astoria, I was scared, but I didn't scream. When I was a child, my night terrors had been so bad that I had slept with the overhead light on. In the Rosebriar Inn, when I could finally move, I got up and went to the bathroom, where I flicked on the light.

I told myself that ghosts don't like the light.

But I was no longer that young girl who slept with an overhead light, and the bathroom light kept me from falling asleep. Finally I pushed Caleb awake. "Will you go and turn off the bathroom light?" I asked. I was too scared to do it myself.

He grumbled, "Why did you turn on the light in the first place?" Still, he got up and turned off the light.

I didn't say, "Because I was afraid."

THE NEXT MORNING, he teased me over breakfast, and finally I said, "I thought that I saw a ghost, okay? I was scared." He laughed at me, and then I said, "She was a woman, and I think she had been abused by her husband. I know it sounds crazy, but it felt so real." He had no reaction to the fact that the woman I had dreamed of was being abused.

I didn't tell him that I had felt that fist crack on my own skull, that I had felt her pain.

Caleb was used to my ghosts by then. In our first apartment I had dreamed of that woman—bloated and bruised— floating in the corner of the bedroom. But in the Rosebriar Inn, he teased me, and then we had sex in the shower. As I came, I felt that someone was watching me through the glass door, and Caleb later said that he had felt the same.

AFTER WE DRESSED, we explored town, went to a coffee shop and read our books side by side, walked down to the wharf and looked at the sea lions, and then bought a picnic lunch. Then we drove down the coast to Ecola State Park, where we started our hike down to the ocean. Halfway down the trail, we stopped to eat our lunch while we watched the ocean crash upon the shore. I had grown up landlocked. The immensity of the water thrilled me.

When we reached the beach, we were alone. It was early evening, and the sun shimmered gold on the water. We scooped up sand dollars like delicate flowers. We chased each other.

We took a self-portrait, and it remains my favorite picture

of the two of us: my head bent toward his. Both of us relaxed. The ocean stretching behind us.

Just off to the side was a cave, and I stared at it—the arresting darkness inside it. I wanted to go inside, but I didn't.

The tide was coming in, and I was afraid of drowning.

CALEB AND I went back to our room for our last night in Astoria. I still felt the presence of that woman, but I had made peace with her and slept soundly that night. The next morning, after breakfast, as I was readying for a shower, Caleb rushed into the room. "Let's go," he said, scooping our clothes into our suitcase.

"I was just getting ready for a shower," I said.

"Shower tomorrow," he said. "I'm ready to get on the road."

We went downstairs to check out of the inn, and while the woman at the counter was preparing our bill, Caleb said, "I have something to show you." He took me to a table in the lobby. There was a little book on it titled *Haunted Astoria*. It was a book written by a ghost-hunting agency. "Turn to the chapter on the Rosebriar Inn," he said. A medium who had been brought in to investigate had said that the room we had stayed in was haunted by the ghost of a woman who was "afraid for him to come home."

I laughed. "I guess I'm psychic," I said, tossing down the book.

"Honestly, it freaks me out," Caleb said. I realized that was why he had wanted to leave so quickly.

"Honey," I said, "if there is really a ghost in there, she was there the entire time. I don't think leaving sooner makes a difference now, but this is going to make a really great story."

It did make a great story, and in the years that followed, I thought of that woman often. At the time, I had never known what a fist to the head felt like, but Caleb would show me.

I learned about "old hag syndrome," where the victim wakes to the feeling that a woman is pressing down on her chest. It's just another word for sleep paralysis, but the victim feels haunted. I knew that what I had experienced was a dream, but still the idea of that woman remained coiled inside me. What if she *had* been a ghost? What if she had come to warn me? What if she had been a ghost from my own future?

When I woke to that woman's presence on my chest, I didn't yet know that the memory of Caleb's fist would become a ghost in my bones.

Caleb and I drove down the coast to Corvallis, Oregon, where we spent a couple of days with Megan and her husband. We stopped along the way at a shipwreck. Caleb took a picture of me in front of the boat's hollowed-out skeleton. When I looked at the picture, I thought that though I was smiling, I looked sad.

We headed back to Boise, where my parents had been taking good care of Reed. He stretched his arms out to me, and I buried my head in his warm baby softness. I had never been sentimental with my parents before. We didn't have that kind of relationship, but I cried this time as their car drove away. In only a month, Caleb, Reed, and I would be leaving them behind, on our way to West Virginia.

I thought that we were doing the right thing.

MY IN-LAWS CAME to help us move. We packed all our belongings into boxes, then hired a moving van to take them cross-country. Caleb and his father were driving our car to West Virginia, and Joanne and I were flying together. Caleb left, and Joanne and I were alone in the house with Reed during that final day. Joanne entertained Reed while I scrubbed everything clean. I didn't know how to talk to her, and I felt so sad. At one point she took Reed to the store, and I sat in the middle of the empty living room and wept.

We boarded the plane the next day. Reed sat on my lap as we took off, and Joanne sat a couple of rows behind us. I wished that it was my own mother with me. As the plane rose higher, I saw the brown desert of the Boise foothills below me, then the peaks of the Rocky Mountains, and soon the plains of the Midwest stretched before me.

"Goodbye, Idaho," I whispered. "I'll be home soon."

14

Christmas Baby

ON A FRIGID white Christmas in Idaho—just across the border from Wyoming, in the same snowy town where my father had started his first job with the US Forest Service, where my mother had once slid into a snowbank in her Volkswagen Bug, and my brother, still a tot, had panicked and jumped out of the car into that bank—I was born. My brother's fifth Christmas was effectively ruined, and though my parents called me the best Christmas gift they'd ever received, it was always in the back of my mind. I was not a Christmas gift; I was the one who ruined Christmas.

IN ASTROLOGY, THOSE born under the sign of Capricorn are austere. Winter babies are born into darkness.

IN THE FIRST or second grade, I grew so impatient to know what I was getting for Christmas that I ripped open every single package under the Christmas tree. First I opened my own, and then the disappointment set in—the realization that I had nothing left to look forward to—so I opened everyone else's presents too. My mother was enraged. I cowered in the corner of my bedroom as she screamed at me, and I knew that I was bad.

Always, I was bad.

That year, I received a plastic baggie of coal in my stocking. My father looked at my mother and laughed. It should have been funny, *was* funny, but I was hurt. I still believed in Santa. I thought that, in addition to disappointing my parents, I had also disappointed Santa. My father stopped laughing when he saw my face. He looked at my mother as though to say, *Maybe we went too far.* My mother gently took the baggie out of my hands and said, "Look at the rest. You still got everything you wanted." But what I had really wanted was to be a good girl.

IN 2004 MY mother's brother died on Christmas Eve, and she flew to Texas. My father, brother, and I spent that Christmas alone. I had started dating Caleb during that October, and he was in West Virginia, visiting his family.

Before Caleb left for West Virginia, I asked him, "Can I call you my boyfriend?"

He kissed me quickly. "Yes," he said.

"So, we're not seeing other people?"

"No, I only want to see you."

I drove him to the airport at dawn. The sun was rising, and the Boise foothills were bathed in light. On my way home, I thought, I think I love him. But then: Something does not feel right.

Still, as I tucked myself back under the covers for a couple more hours of sleep, all I could remember was how much warmer my bed had been with him inside it.

WHILE HE WAS away, Caleb sent me a card for my birthday. He wrote, "My mom didn't get the joke, but I know that you will get it." And I did get it. It was an inside joke. The card had a honeybee on the cover. On the inside, it said, "Love you, HONEY." The joke stemmed from the time when I told Caleb about a romance novel I read in the eighth grade. A pirate said to his love, "I've tasted your milk. Now I want to taste your honey." I read that line out loud to my girlfriends in the middle of science lab, and we howled with laughter. At that time, I read so many romance novels that my mother finally went to the public library and asked them to stop checking them out to me. She told me they would give me "unrealistic expectations" of love.

My mother was right. They did give me unrealistic expectations about love.

AFTER I TOLD Caleb that story, he leaned in to kiss my neck—his beard tickling me—and growled into my ear, "I want to taste your honey."

"That's so creepy!" I said, but then I laughed and turned my face to him so that he could kiss me properly. It became a ritual. He would sneak up on me from behind and whisper that he wanted to "taste my honey." The feel of his beard on my neck always startled me, but in the most delightful way.

ON THAT CHRISTMAS in 2004 when my uncle died, Caleb called. My father said, "There's a guy on the phone for you," while shooting me a curious glance because I hadn't said much to my parents about a new boyfriend. Caleb then told me about how embarrassed he had been to ask his mother for a ride to get my birthday card. I said, "Why did you need a ride? Why couldn't you drive yourself?" I didn't know at the time that his driver's license was suspended in West Virginia because of a DUI. He didn't tell me that until after we married. Instead, he distracted me by saying, "My family all wanted to know about you. I told them that you were beautiful, and smart, and funny." I told him about my uncle's death and realized how little we knew about each other.

I WENT BACK to Boise after that Christmas in 2004. Caleb was still in West Virginia. One night I accompanied some friends to the Neurolux. An attractive man—angular face, dark glasses, and dark hair, brooding and slightly older than me—caught my eye. I had caught him staring at me many times before. I had told my friends how cute I thought he was. That night he came and sat next to me.

We talked, and he was interesting—an artist and musician. He seemed kind. I said nothing about Caleb. I let the man walk me home. I let him into my apartment. I put on some music. He said, "You have good taste in music."

He said, "I have been noticing you for a while." I told him that I had been noticing him too. Then he kissed me, and I kissed him back.

Not for long, but for a moment.

I pulled away and said, "I'm so sorry, but I am seeing someone. It's really new, but we just decided that we're going to only see each other. I should have said something sooner."

He pulled back, looked into his lap, then back up. "You're a really good person," he said. He looked away, then said, "Things don't always work out. If they don't, you know how to find me, okay?"

"Okay," I said.

"I mean that," he said.

Then he got up and left. I sat on my couch in the darkness. Part of me hoped that I would get that chance.

I TOLD CALEB about that man, about letting him kiss me. Caleb said, "Why are you telling me this?"

"I just want to be honest," I responded.

"Thank you," he said, and I congratulated myself on our openness with each other. I didn't know then that at that exact same time, he had been having sex with a high school friend.

A year later, in 2005, Caleb and I were married. Reed was a newborn. We slept in my childhood bedroom. Reed slept in a bassinet by the bed. He sighed. He made smacking noises. I woke, and my breasts ached. Milk leaked from my nipples. Caleb and I got through it by laughing. We joked about how long it had been since we'd had sex. I can't remember how it came up. I said, "I haven't had sex with anyone else since we started dating." Caleb was silent. I turned to him in the darkness. "Why? Have you?" I was more curious than angry. More silence from Caleb.

"No," he said. "Of course not."

IT WASN'T UNTIL Reed was over a year old that I started to find out about all the others. The secrets always came out over a long period of time. Never all at once. I kept picking. He finally broke. It wasn't so much the fact that he had been with other women when we were dating, but the cruelty with which he described them.

WE WERE IN the car in the driveway of my parents' house. I stared at the light glowing out of the windows. Smoke drifted from the chimney into the darkness. I wanted to run away. I wanted to scream.

He apologized.

Begged.

Maybe even cried.

I couldn't look at him.

I went into the house. "There's my baby," I whispered, picking toddler Reed up and blowing a bubble on his stomach.

AND THEN, ON a Christmas Eve in 2009—five years after that Christmas in 2004—there was this.

And isn't *this* what this story is really about?

CALEB HIT ME. Fist connected with scalp. The meal cooled while Caleb screamed at me in the kitchen, and then his fist punched into my head. I felt not pain but relief. Now, I thought, he will get this out of his system and *he will finally stop*. But he didn't stop. He never stopped. We finally ate the lamb roast and risotto cakes that I had made.

I ate with my face swollen from tears and fist.

I said, "Isn't this good?"

He said, "Merry Christmas."

I said, "Thank you."

I DIDN'T ENJOY Christmas with Caleb's family, and he knew it. His family was large and insular, and I didn't feel that I belonged. I felt that his mother cared more about getting a beautiful scrapbook page out of the holiday than actually having a beautiful holiday.

Caleb and I had planned our own private celebration for Christmas Eve because we were driving to his family's on Christmas Day. I had made a fig-stuffed lamb roast, risotto cakes, and roasted brussels sprouts.

Unbeknownst to me, Kelly M. had been doing her own planning. She secretly reached out to all of our friends. She told them that my birthday was on Christmas, that I had never had a proper birthday, that I had never even had classroom cupcakes. She told them I was going to have to spend my birthday on the floor of my sister-in-law's house, and that she wanted to come up with enough money to get me a hotel room in the fanciest hotel in town. Our friends came through, and she called me with excitement on Christmas Eve to tell me that she had come up with enough money to get Caleb and me a room at the Blennerhassett Hotel. I was so touched, and Caleb had known about her efforts all along. He said, "That's so sweet of Kelly M," he said. "This is great, baby."

BUT THAT NIGHT, as I bustled around the kitchen, I felt his anger growing. I didn't know where it was coming from, so I grew anxious. I offered him compliments, I offered him food and wine. I hugged him and felt his shoulders rigid under my hands. By then, I knew what his silence and tense body meant.

Finally he exploded, "How could you humiliate me like this?"

I was confused, had no idea what he was talking about. "What do you mean?" I asked.

"How could you tell Kelly that you didn't want to stay at my sister's house?"

"I didn't," I protested. "I never said anything like that. I love staying at your sister's house. You know that."

And then he bellowed, "You don't respect me!"

I ran into the living room to get away from him. He followed. He backed me up against the wall. "I didn't say anything to Kelly," I whispered. But he was so close, so angry.

Finally I couldn't take it anymore. I shouted, "Just do it! You know that you want to."

He threw me to the ground. Was on top of me. He screamed over and over again, "Is this what you want? Is this what you want? Is this what you want?"

The blows kept coming.

By then, it *was* what I wanted.

When he was finished, I curled into a ball. Maybe this will be what makes him finally stop scaring me, I thought. Maybe he will finally realize he has gone too far.

WHEN I WAS a kid, I was always jealous of my brother. I felt that he was the favorite. Once I counted all of his Christmas presents, and all of mine. He had twice as many as I did, and I presented the evidence to my parents. They rationally presented me with the counterevidence: my brother and I were different ages, and not all presents are of the same monetary value.

Still, for some reason, I thought that love could be measured in presents. I didn't know how to measure love in less tangible ways.

Once, while Caleb and I were visiting my family for Christmas, he, my brother, and I went to a party at a friend's house. Caleb left early, and my brother and I walked home together. He didn't know how unhappy I was in my marriage. We talked about our childhoods, and my brother said, "I don't think that we experienced the same things." I started crying unexpectedly, and he hugged me on that dark sidewalk. I sobbed into his chest. I knew that I was not only sobbing about my childhood, but I couldn't articulate what I was feeling. I said, "You were always the favorite."

He said, "That's true, but you were always the smart one. Would you have rather been the favorite?"

I thought of that for a while, then sniffled. "No," I said.

"I know," he said.

I wiped my face with my sleeve, and we walked home in the cold December darkness.

CALEB ALWAYS GAVE me the most thoughtful presents. Things that he knew I would love. If I liked something, it would eventually end up wrapped and in front of me. I had no interest in trends or expensive things. I didn't want diamonds or a fancy purse. I wanted earrings made by a local artisan, leather earrings with beads on them. A large, red stone pendant necklace. A trio of prints made by an artist we knew. Or a book written by my favorite author.

Holidays with him were fraught—a mixture of joy and tension. He was a thoughtful gift giver, a wonderful cook, an attentive father, but the stress of travel combined with familial expectations induced his anger. If I asked him for help with the house or getting Reed ready for our travels, Caleb would scream at me that I didn't appreciate all that he did for me. He would bring up what he had cooked, the presents that he had bought for me. He would scream, "I give you everything you want, and it's never enough."

I remembered myself as the little girl who had counted her presents. I saw myself as greedy, always wanting too much. I grew to dread Christmas.

AFTER CALEB BEAT me on that Christmas Eve, I had to wear long sleeves to his parents' house. At one point, I forgot. I pushed up my sleeve in the kitchen. My sister-in-law reached out for my arm. "What happened?" she asked, her voice soft and low. How could I have ever told her? I don't remember how I answered. There would be so many more questions like that in the years to come.

THAT CHRISTMAS, BACK in 2005, Caleb and I walked our dog down by the river in Salmon. Our dog ran out onto that ice and slid into the river. I screamed. Caleb stretched out on the thin ice. He grabbed our dog's paws and pulled him out.

Reed was five weeks old.

As Caleb stretched onto the ice, I thought, I am going to be raising my child alone. But though the ice shook and heaved, it didn't break. The black water ran beneath it— hard, and fast, and cold.

15

What I Didn't Write

I FOLLOWED THE CHRISTMAS letter tradition in a family blog that spanned a couple of years. But these posts had a way of leaving out the bad stuff. There was so much that I didn't write.

WHAT I DID WRITE.

I wrote about how much Reed loved living near his cousins. I wrote that Reed named everyone in relationship to himself. That his cousin was the "best friend of Reed."

I wrote that I was the "mommy of Reed."

I WROTE THAT I knew that Reed would likely be an only child. I wrote about how much older my brother was than me—how I had often felt like an only child—and how my cousins had all grown up across the country from me. I wrote that I wanted to give Reed a different childhood from the one I had.

I wrote that, as much as I liked Morgantown, I missed the West and wanted to return to my home.

I wrote that I had received an award for being the top creative-writing undergraduate in the department, that I was starting to think of myself as a writer.

I wrote that we had bought our first home.

I wrote that Caleb's friend who was a police officer often visited when he was on shift. I wrote about how the neighbors seemed to judge us because the cops were always coming to our house. I wrote that I thought that was funny.

I wrote about our bumper crop of heirloom tomatoes—how easy it was to grow tomatoes in the rich West Virginia soil. I wrote about how fall was approaching, and I dreaded the way the leaves would fall, just after they had turned so beautiful—the way the beauty of those autumn leaves signaled the beginning of the long winter.

I wrote that West Virginia winters were lonely.

I wrote that Caleb was teaching too many classes, that he had to commute on the snowy roads and I worried about him.

I wrote that we didn't get to see my parents enough.

I wrote about how, in a last-ditch effort to save summer, we went to a family-friendly bluegrass joint in Thomas, West Virginia. We took Reed to see a bluegrass band, and then we went back to our room and watched the original *Willy Wonka and the Chocolate Factory* on an old VHS machine. Reed had his own little twin bed, and he would sit up and wave at us while yelling "Hi Mommy! Hi Daddy!" Then he would grin ear to ear, stick his thumb in his mouth, and lie back down.

I wrote that, on that same trip, we went to the Dolly Sods Wilderness for a picnic and hike. The elevation was high enough that I could almost convince myself I was in Idaho. I wrote that we had found a bog full of huckleberries and wild blueberries. We picked as many as we could without straying off the trail because the Dolly Sods had been a live training area during World War II, and there were still live bombs there.

I wrote that Reed ate as many blueberries and huckleberries as he could pick, that he ran up and down the trail laughing, that I had to watch out for him because he didn't know that there was danger buried underneath all of that beauty.

I wrote that Kelly M. had launched a fund-raising effort to get me a hotel room for my birthday, but that Caleb and I had used the hotel credit later and gone to Pittsburgh for a weekend instead. I wrote that we had gone to the Andy Warhol Museum, eaten at a brew pub in a converted church, and had dinner with Caleb's friends.

I wrote that the university paid for us to go to Greece for a week, so that Caleb could prepare to teach a class on Greece. I wrote that we got lost looking for the cave where Socrates was held prisoner.

I wrote that I had decided to be impractical and follow my dreams rather than get the MA in teaching English as a second language. I wrote that I was accepted to WVU's MFA program. I wrote that when the director called me, he told me I was their top candidate.

I wrote that I was afraid of failing.

I wrote that Caleb and I had some of the same students, and they all seemed to love him. I wrote that one of my students had come to my office, and Caleb had brought me lunch while she was there. When he left, she said, "That is so awesome that you two are married. You are my favorite teachers."

I WROTE ABOUT my health problems—the weight gain, insulin resistance, sleep issues, high blood pressure.

I wrote that I had found it difficult to make friends in Morgantown, that I missed Kelly M. and my other friends, that I felt isolated

AND THEN I stopped writing on that blog.

I stopped writing because what I wasn't writing was becoming too large to ignore. I stopped writing because it was becoming impossible to rewrite the story in a way that felt authentic.

I stopped writing because I wanted to write, "I no longer know where he ends, and I begin."

I stopped writing because I wanted to write, "He ends."

I stopped writing because I wanted to write, "I begin."

16

A Hard Heart

MY MARRIAGE WASN'T like the romance novels I read in middle school, where the men were withholding and angry at first, but always became gentle and nurturing by the end. It was more like an after-school special where the men were gentle and nurturing at first, but withholding and angry by the end. I was heartbroken, but even more than that, Caleb's anger taught me to be hard. My rage filled the house; it became the fourth family member. When I was playing with Reed, I became Happy Mommy. Happy Mommy wants to play peekaboo. Happy Mommy wants to hear your story. Happy Mommy wants to go for a walk. Happy Mommy wants to cuddle you to sleep.

But I had a monster inside. At night I curled next to Caleb, my body outlining his contours, my hand caressing his head, our way of falling asleep. But my heart always said, *I won't forgive.*

BY THE TIME Caleb first hit me, I no longer understood where right ended and wrong began. At the time, I was thriving in graduate school—had bonded with my graduate adviser and was winning competitive awards—and my writing was going well. Caleb was also working hard to gain some recognition as a writer. Perhaps there was some unspoken competition between us, but I was always proud of his efforts, and he knew that. When we were dating, I had gone to a graduate reading of his at a coffee shop. His story was about boys in the woods of Appalachia. There was an angry preacher who taught the main character to feel shame, and at the end of the story, the boys burn the forest down. The main character, a boy who sounded a lot like Caleb, stands in the middle of the fire and watches it burn.

With his clean-shaven face, he looked so young and tender as he read his brutal story. For years he would tell me that he had felt so strong, reading in front of that crowd, my face glowing with pride at the front of the room.

HE SUBMITTED THAT story to almost one hundred journals. Years later, it was finally published in a decent journal that his mother prominently displayed in her living room. Privately, she told me, "That story was so dark. I didn't raise him like that."

I thought, You don't get him.

That lapse was one of the reasons why throughout our marriage, I never felt comfortable in the home of my in-laws. When we visited, I would fatigue from all of the activity, the pressure. Sometimes I would escape to the upstairs bathroom. Once I saw Caleb's mother's Bible sitting on the counter. I opened it to a random page, and read a passage.

They shall not pour libations of
wine to the Lord;
and they shall not please him
with their sacrifices
Their bread shall be like mourners' bread;
all who eat of it shall be defiled;
for their bread shall be for their hunger only.

I heard those words repeat in my head, and later, I wrote an essay about love, shame, failure, and forgiveness. I felt the hardness in my heart softening. I titled it "Like Mourners' Bread." In the essay, I was mostly honest about Caleb's treatment of me, but the physical abuse was still rare, and I thought that it was going to remain that way.

The ending was about the importance of forgiveness. I believed my own words. I believed that my forgiveness was the key to our healing. I believed that my hard heart was perpetuating our misery.

When Caleb read "Like Mourners' Bread," he said, "It's beautiful. It hurts to read, but I know that it's true. I know that I didn't treat you right, and you have every reason to tell this story."

I felt valued. As a writer. As a wife. As a person.

I thought, How many women have a husband who supports their career so fully that they can write painful truths about him, and he is okay with that?

I REMEMBERED HOW many times my mother had said to me, "You and Caleb have something special. You have so much in common. That is not easy to find. Don't give up on that."

When I won the prestigious award in my graduate program, Caleb and I were at my parents' house for Christmas, and my mother said to me, "Your father is always so surprised by how easily you can write things!"

We were all in the living room together—my mother, father, Caleb, and me. The fireplace was burning, and the Christmas tree glowed in the corner. Caleb jumped in, and he said, "It isn't easy for her. She works really hard. Kelly has achieved what she has because of her hard work."

I thought that Caleb was my best ally. Even when we were out in social situations, Caleb would say proudly, "If anyone in this family ever makes money off their writing, it's going to be Kelly, and I'm okay with that."

AROUND THE TIME that I wrote "Like Mourners' Bread," I saw an advertisement for a writer's conference that was being held by an up-and-coming New York literary magazine. The conference wasn't very expensive, and it had a contest. Only people attending could enter it, and they would publish the winner (who would receive a small cash prize). I had received another scholarship from my department that would pay for my travel to a conference, and I proposed that Caleb and I go together. He got travel funding from his department, and we attended.

We both entered the contest, but I was the one who won.

After getting the news, Caleb took me out for tacos. We

drank margaritas. I saw a pair of really cute boots in a bou-
tique shop in Brooklyn, and he said, "Why don't you use your
winnings to buy those?" Even though I knew we couldn't afford them, I bought the boots. He told everyone how proud
he was of me, and I believed him.

WHEN WE RETURNED home, I was on a high, but Caleb grew
depressed. He lamented how he would never succeed with
a short-story collection. I tried to console him, but nothing
worked. Then, meanwhile, my essays were getting accepted
again and again.

SOON HE WAS hitting me. Each time an acceptance letter arrived, he would brag about how proud he was of me, and there
would usually be a delay of a day or two, but then he would
find a reason to beat me. I didn't make the connection because
I believed his words. Still, my body knew better. Without real-
izing it, I stopped submitting anything for publication.

ONE NIGHT, AFTER Caleb had gone to bed and I was still
awake with insomnia, I had a breakdown. I punched the
couch. I screamed—internally, because Caleb and Reed
were sleeping—*I would give it all up if Caleb could just have one
success*. I meant it. By then, I would have given anything up
for his happiness, because his unhappiness was breaking me.

WHEN I GRADUATED from my MFA program, the department held a final reading where the graduates invited their

family and friends. I had no friends or family in Morgan-town, so I asked my in-laws to come. At first they declined, but then Caleb came to me and said, "My mom is going to drive up for the night, and then back. She wants to be there for the reading."

"Did you ask her to do this?" I asked.

"No," he said. "She wanted to do it on her own." But I knew that he had told her I had been hurt. I knew that as my biggest ally, he had my back.

I tried to find an essay to read that didn't feel too personal, too raw. I finally settled on an excerpt, but was embarrassed when I saw how uncomfortable Joanne was in the audience. Like my own mother, she was so very private. Who was I to share all of my secrets?

My own parents came on graduation day. My mother took a photo of me in my cap and gown with Caleb; I had never seen my parents so proud of me. I felt that, maybe, I had finally earned their approval, finally proven to them that I could finish something.

IN THE WEEK before my graduation, Caleb had interviewed for a position as a resident faculty leader in one of the dormitories on campus. It was a fairly prestigious position, and because Caleb was not on a tenure track, if he got it, it would completely change our financial situation. Still, the position involved moving into a dormitory, and I didn't know how I felt about that.

As soon as my parents left, Caleb and I resumed fighting.

Over everything. Over nothing. One of the fights got so bad that, in a rage, I threw my coffee mug at the wall. Caleb picked it up off the floor and reared his arm back. He threw the mug at me, and it landed on my leg. The pain shattered me, grounding me to the couch. Caleb picked the mug up again.

I curled up on the couch, wrapped my arms around my legs. I begged him to stop.

No. It hurts.

He gave a little smile. Reared his arm back as though he was pitching a baseball. He had been an All-Star.

"No!" I screamed. He threw the mug at me, and it shattered against my elbow. I blacked out for a moment from the pain. When I woke, I saw that my elbow had swollen to the size of a softball.

I don't remember what happened after that.

WE WENT FOR a joint interview with the assistant provost and the resident director of the dormitory. It was a hot and humid day, so I wore a light sweater that ended at my elbows. I smiled. I chatted. I saw the resident director looking curiously at my elbow, which was still swollen large and almost black. I pulled down my sleeve.

At the end of the interview, the assistant provost asked the resident director how he felt about working with us, and the resident director responded, "I feel great." He left, and she made us a formal offer.

She said, "I liked Caleb, but now that I've met you, Kelly,

I know that I'm making the right decision. I envision you as his equal. You will be the perfect partners for this position."

I WAS EXCITED, but scared. I couldn't stop thinking of that coffee mug breaking on my elbow, but how could I leave? I was a recent graduate with an MFA. I didn't even have a job, and I knew I would never be able to support Reed on my own. I needed to try and make things work with Caleb, and he had promised me that he would change.

HE HAD STARTED getting anger management therapy, and had brought home a list of the types of angry men. One of them was the Hero. The Hero had been so valued by his family that he couldn't possibly live up to their expectations. The anger came because he had been told to expect a charmed life that bore no resemblance to the life he was actually living. The Hero lived in constant fear of disappointing his loved ones. Maybe the resident faculty leader was a hero's position. Maybe Caleb could finally be happy.

BEFORE WE MOVED into the dormitory, Caleb and I sat in our backyard and watched a lunar eclipse. The moon moved so slowly I could track it with my eyes, Caleb's tender gaze beside mine.

I surrendered to the beauty.

I prayed.

I begged.

Save me.

I feared that it was a bad idea to move into the dormitory, but wasn't it a worse idea not to? Maybe I would finally be safe there.

As I was praying, the moon moved behind the earth's shadow, and Caleb reached his hand across the distance between us. His fingers grasped mine, and the darkness obliterated the light.

17

The Archivist

IN A TOWN built on a hill, in a state full of sawed-off mountains where muddy roads curved along polluted streams, metal deposits in the water gleamed like steely rainbows, and the muted sunlight filtered through shadowy trees, there lived an archivist. His was a job of remembrance.

Mine was a job of forgetting.

ON HIS PHONE, Caleb had begun keeping a collection of self-portraits. In them, he stared into the camera. Somber. Almost frightening. He told me that he took the photos to catalog his shame. If the photos created an archive of his shame, then they archived my shame too.

When I saw his misery documented in photo after photo, I wondered how the person I loved could be so unhappy with me. It was as if the violence that was my fault was causing him more suffering than it was causing me.

WE HAD MOVED into the dorm—a sleek twelve-story modernist building that had been recently renovated. The apartment we lived in was larger than the house we owned, with dark-brown hardwood floors, leather furniture, a long mahogany table that could seat twelve, and a kitchen with shining stainless-steel appliances, granite countertops, and tiny pearl pendants that cast light over the counters. The back of the house was equally glamorous, with lush carpet and new paint.

The assistant provost had encouraged us to make the apartment our own—to hang up our own art, and put our own books in the bookshelves—but everything that we owned seemed so cheap in comparison. We easily filled the bookshelves, then hung some prints that I had recently brought home from a visit to Vietnam for Kelly M.'s wedding. We also hung the golden Vietnamese wedding bells that I had shaken after Kelly M. and her husband said their vows.

Kelly's mother had paid for my plane ticket to Vietnam, so I could be a part of the ceremony, which was held on the shore of a deep blue reservoir in the Vietnamese mountains, and Kelly had asked me to read a quote from bell hooks about love being a verb. I fought back tears as I read the words, because I no longer believed that my own marriage was going to last.

I HAD HOPED that I would be safe in the apartment in the dorm, but that didn't turn out to be the case. Caleb's rages continued, and the memories of his violence became a part of my body that I tried to forget. Once the resident director was visiting with us in our apartment. He was a kind but animated person, and he slammed his hand onto the granite countertop for emphasis. The loud noise startled me into sudden shivers. I looked at the resident director, who didn't realize how he had scared me, and the words *Help me* swelled within my mouth, but my lips remained closed.

THE VIOLENCE HAD been so slow to come on, but suddenly, it came fast.

WHEN WE LIVED in our own house, I could leave when Caleb scared me. I was a regular at the Travelodge, but I always returned home before morning, keeping the hotel key card just in case, then climbing into bed and wrapping my arms around Caleb's back. I didn't want Reed to wake up and find me gone, and I still loved Caleb. *In sickness, and in health.* Those were my vows in that little church in Idaho where we held hands while sunlight filtered through stained glass and spring lilacs bloomed outside. I told myself that Caleb was sick, but he would get better.

AT THE DORM, I couldn't escape to the Travelodge. Someone would notice. They would wonder what was wrong. No longer could I get away before Caleb hit me.

In our bedroom, there was a walk-in closet where I used to hide while he raged. I would climb behind the suitcases stuffed into one corner. I knew he would find me, but I would hide anyway. If I hid underneath the bed, he would drag me out by my ankles. Usually he punched me in the head—and because I wrapped my arms around my hair, there would sometimes be visible bruises on my arms. They were easy to hide. Once I forgot to wear long sleeves. The students had come over to the apartment for a writing workshop that my friend Rebecca was leading. I reached for something, and Rebecca touched my arm—so gently. Her eyes looked horrified. "What happened?" she asked, nodding at the large black bruise on my forearm. Caleb stood there, watchful. I panicked. I wasn't a good liar.

"I don't know," I said. "I think I must have done it in my sleep."

ANOTHER TIME, I had lunch with Rebecca, and my hand was black and swollen. "I closed it in the door," I said. "I am so clumsy." She didn't question me. No one questioned Caleb's devotion to me. They only ever thought that we were happy.

HE ONLY HIT me in the face once. We were in the bathroom, and he was screaming at me. I had a bottle of Ambien on the counter. He grabbed it and held it to my closed lips. He sawed away at the tender redness, slicing my skin with the rough plastic of the bottle. Finally, I gave in. Opened my mouth and let him pour the pills in my mouth. I was ready to swallow them if that was what he wanted. I was ready to give up.

I held the pills in my cheeks. I didn't have much to live for, but I didn't want to die. Didn't want to leave my child. My eyes begged Caleb, and he punched me in the face, causing the pills to spit out across the floor. "You're fucking crazy," he said.

I felt fucking crazy.

Then he was calm. We both sat on the bathroom floor, exhausted. A red bruise bloomed across my cheek, and my lip was cut open from the pill bottle. My eye was also split and oozing. "You made me hit you in the face," he said mournfully. "Now everyone is going to know."

"I know," I said. "I'm sorry."

I THOUGHT I was losing my hair from stress. In the shower, red strands swam in the water by my feet. Chunks were stuck to my fingers. It didn't matter. I hadn't felt pretty in years.

When I rubbed the shampoo into my scalp, the skin was tender, and I realized I wasn't losing my hair. He had ripped it out, and I hadn't even felt it.

I WENT INTO a cave when he hit me, wrapped my arms around my body and *left*.

I WAS ONLY ever *leaving*. I was *leaving* when he hit me. *Leaving* when he screamed "You are a fucking cunt!" at me. *Leaving* when he threw the coffee mug at me. *Leaving* when he chased me into the other room. *Leaving* when I ran into Reed's room because I knew that Caleb would never hit me in front of his son. Reed, seemingly oblivious, always knew to go to his room during Caleb's rages.

I was *leaving*, but never gone.

STILL, WHEN WE lay in bed, Reed between us, my head on Caleb's shoulder, his head resting on mine, and Reed said

"The whole family is cuddled up"—when that happened, I was there. I felt that love. I felt it all.

I needed to try more things.

An Incomplete List of the Things We Tried

1. **Visualization** *(me)*. I watched an *Oprah* special on manifestation that said that, in order to make something happen, I had to pretend as if it had already happened. One way of doing this was offering up gratitude to the universe, so I started writing thank-you lists.

   Thank you for my beautiful son. Thank you for Reed's health. Thank you for Caleb's understanding of me. Thank you for Caleb's humor. Thank you for Caleb's book getting published. Thank you for Caleb getting a tenure-track job. Thank you for Caleb's happiness.

   It didn't occur to me to offer up gratitude for myself because by then, I thought the path to my own happiness was through Caleb's.

2. **Mindfulness** *(me)*. I read a book that instructed me to focus on the present moment. Was I suffering in that moment? If not, then I needed to release my worries.

   Mindfulness worked. Once, I sat in my car at an intersection, and suddenly the memory of Caleb's fist shattered into my awareness. My breathing quickened, and I thought about how I needed to leave him. But then I settled into my present body. Was I suffering in that moment? There at that intersection? I wasn't. Not really.

According to the book, if I was ruminating on past deeds, I was creating my own suffering and needed to let it go. In that particular way, letting go of my suffering seemed easy enough, because most of the time, Caleb wasn't hitting me.

When he was hitting me, I wasn't present enough to focus on mindfulness anyway.

The same book claimed that we all have a "pain-body"—an autonomous manifestation of our psychic pain—that wants to antagonize other peoples' pain-bodies. I read the theory to Caleb, and later, when we would argue, he would dismiss my concerns. "That's just your pain-body trying to pick a fight," he would say.

When he hit me, I would tell myself, *It's not Caleb. It's just his pain-body expressing itself.*

3. **Watching porn** *(Caleb)*. Caleb was looking at Internet pornography all of the time. I went to a writer's conference, and while I was gone, he called in sick to work so that he could look at pornography for hours at a time. I found out because when I got home and we tried to have sex, we couldn't. I pressed him about what was wrong, and he finally admitted it.

When I confided what was happening to my friends—but not in full detail because that would have humiliated him—they said, "This is normal. Everyone looks at por-nography." I knew this was true. I felt that something was wrong with me. I was just insecure. Jéalous. I was the one with the problem.

Sometimes, in the middle of the night, Caleb would wake and leave our bedroom—tell me he couldn't sleep—and he would go downstairs to watch pornography. At the time, I wouldn't know what he was doing, but the bed would feel empty without him.

Sometimes, late at night, I would pull up the computer screen, and there they were: these women.

A woman being raped in an elevator.

A woman lying on the floor crying while a circle of men ejaculated on her.

A woman with a man holding her hair while jamming her face into his crotch and yelling, Do you like this? Do you like this?

A woman crying, I like it. I like it.

4. **Individual counseling** (*me*). I didn't tell her that Caleb hit me because I didn't think his hitting me was the problem. I talked about Caleb's pornography use, and she gave me a referral to a counselor for Caleb to see. Things seemed better when Caleb started seeing his counselor, so I stopped seeing my therapist.

Individual counseling (*Caleb*). Caleb's counselor operated a private practice out of his basement. The counselor liked to use props, and he had a tiny children's chair. When a patient would start to rationalize or minimize his behavior, the counselor would make the patient sit in the children's chair until his adult self was ready to speak. Caleb told me that there were sessions when he had to sit in the children's chair the entire time.

5. **Couples counseling** *(both of us)*. Caleb took me with him to see his counselor. At the end of the appointment, the counselor looked at him and said, "Caleb, she is not what you led me to believe she was." I wondered what that meant. I didn't ask Caleb because I didn't want to violate the privacy of his therapy sessions.

6. **Drinking too much** *(Caleb)*. He had always been a problematic drinker, but if he was an alcoholic, he was a functioning one. Still, the summer before the final year of my MFA, I drove to a parking garage and called Jeannie, who, by then, was my only divorced friend. I wept. "I think I need to leave him," I said.

   She told me that maybe it was time, and I drove home. He could tell that I was serious when I walked in the door. "I'm leaving," I said. "I'll get my parents to help me."

   Still, when I called them and said that I wanted to leave my marriage, my mother was silent. I took her silence as disapproval. She didn't offer any help. Soon thereafter, Caleb promised to change in every way possible and actually quit drinking.

   He got his thirty-day chip from AA, then cracked a beer.

7. **Drinking too much** *(both of us)*. Once Caleb looked at me and said sadly, "We only like each other when we're drinking."

8. **Anger management** *(Caleb)*. Caleb said that his counselor wasn't helping him enough with his anger. He needed

someone who specialized in anger. He found a man named Dan who worked in a methadone clinic. Caleb's abuse of me got worse. He started bringing me articles about women with personality disorders who antagonized their husbands because they were addicted to chaos.

Once Caleb came home from an appointment with Dan and raged at me. I cried, "Why do you seem worse since you've started seeing Dan?"

Caleb looked at me, eyes hard. "Because Dan makes me feel good about myself and has taught me that I don't need to take your shit," he said.

9. **Medication** (*both of us*). I took Lexapro (for my anxiety) and Ambien (for my sleep problems). At night I would take the Ambien and feel my body relaxing into sleep. Some mornings I woke up and realized that Caleb and I had sex the night before, but I couldn't remember it.

A psychiatrist prescribed Zoloft for Caleb, and it seemed to help at first, but when the abuse became frequent, I begged him to tell the psychiatrist what was happening. The psychiatrist kept increasing his dosage until it was at the maximum. Caleb kept hitting me.

10. **Working too hard** (*both of us*). I taught classes, completed an MFA, wrote a full collection of essays. Work was my release.

Caleb taught five or six classes a semester. Work was his prison.

11. **Meditation** (*Caleb*). Dan had recommended that Caleb meditate as a way of managing his anger. Caleb set up a

pillow in the corner and sat cross-legged, hands resting on his knees, soft palms facing heavenward.

12. **Moving into the dorm** *(both of us).* One morning I came out of the bedroom and found Caleb meditating underneath a sunny window. I could see the tendons in his neck bulging. Arms furiously tight. Back straight. I knew what was coming, started shivering. He only meditated when he was angry.

Morgantown existed in a rain shadow, and sunny days were rare. I thought of Idaho, of the high-country desert, of the vast blue skies, of climbing mountains with my father, who had only ever treated me with gentleness, of wrestling with my brother who had always let me win. Of Danny and his knife. Of that man in the truck. Of the man who held me down for the first time when I didn't want to be held down.

Caleb's eyes opened; he stared at me. I knew that meditation couldn't save him, and it couldn't save me either. I knew that the only thing that could save me was to run.

CALEB AND I went to see his counselor one final time together. By then, Caleb was mostly seeing Dan, and I knew that he hadn't been honest with either of them about what he was doing to me. We sat on the couch, and the words tumbled around in my mind but didn't escape. Finally Caleb's counselor said, "We're almost out of time. Is there anything else we need to discuss?"

I started sobbing and blurted out, "He's just so mean to me." Even then, I couldn't bring myself to confess the violence, because confessing the violence would mean I had to leave.

Caleb's counselor sat up in his chair. He looked at Caleb. "Caleb," he said. "Is that true?" Caleb sat stiffly, nodded his head.

Caleb's counselor sat back. "This is very serious," he said. "We are going to need to talk about this more, but we don't have time today."

As we were walking out, I stopped Caleb's counselor. "Do you have a recommendation for someone I can see?" I asked.

"But you're seeing me," he said.

"I know," I said, "but I want to see someone on my own."

"Okay," he said. "Let me think about it, and I'll get some names to you."

THE NEXT DAY, he sent me an e-mail with the name of a counselor named Liz. He wrote, "I think she'll be able to help you with your issues with your mother." When I read his note, I realized that he had no idea what my issues really were.

I e-mailed Liz, and we scheduled an appointment. A few nights before the appointment, Caleb beat me late at night. After he had fallen asleep, I slipped out of my bed. I sat at the granite counter in the kitchen and opened my laptop. I e-mailed Liz. I told her that I didn't know what to do, and I had to say something before I lost my courage. I told her that my husband was abusing me, and I was scared. When I woke up, there was an e-mail from Liz that said, simply, "Come see me today."

I WENT TO see Liz in Caleb's counselor's office. I sat on the same couch where I had sat with Caleb, and I lifted the sleeves of my sweatshirt. I showed her the bruises on my arms. She sat next to me. She touched the bruises gently—traced her fingertips along the shadows—and I gasped, heaved.

She hugged me, and I cried on her shoulder. When I finally stopped crying, she said, "You needed that, didn't you?"

I told her that I wasn't ready to leave yet—that I only wanted to learn how to keep myself safe while fixing my marriage. She nodded her head. "Okay," she said. "Let's work on fixing your marriage, but what we really need to work on is keeping you safe."

"Okay," I said.

I wanted to be safe. I didn't want the memories of his fists to be a ghost in my bones anymore. I wanted the memories to be just memories.

In time, I thought, I'll be able to forget.

18

It Will Look Like a Sunset

IT WAS THE day of Reed's seventh birthday party—a superhero party—and from the way that Caleb was raging, I could tell what was coming. This time, I ran. I ducked under his arm, opened the door of the apartment, and took off as fast as I could.

I was safe.

Except that he had followed me. He had followed me, even though the resident assistants were there. "Call the police," I cried, but they were young adults. They were confused and did nothing.

Caleb chased me into the street in his socks. Later, he cried on my shoulder in the basement of the dorm. I had already talked to the resident assistants.

I held Caleb as he sobbed. "I fixed it," I said. "I fixed it."

REED HAD PLAYED quietly on his bed. It was what he always did during these rages. He stayed there as long as was needed. I went into the hallway, and Reed followed me. He stood in front of me, and I looked down at him. He reached out hesitantly, put his hands on my stomach, and looked into my eyes. His eyes searched mine, moving back and forth. His eyes searched mine in a way that they never had before. He was growing up, and his eyes disclosed to me that he knew. He knew what was happening.

"Mom?" he asked, still holding me gently, eyes still attached to mine.

"It's okay, sweetie," I said, reaching down to smooth his thick hair over his forehead. "I'm okay."

"I don't like it when the dogs climb into bed with me because they're scared," he said. He looked so much like I had when I was a child, the same strawberry hair and big blue eyes. I thought of myself as a little girl in Idaho, a sensitive little girl who witnessed the sadness of the adults around her, but who never imagined that her own future would contain so much heartbreak. In that moment, I knew. I knew we had to leave.

I CLEANED MYSELF up, put ice on my swollen eyes, and hosted the best birthday party that Reed had ever had. A mess of little superheroes were in our apartment, and I fed them pizza and gave them cupcakes. We took them on a scavenger hunt throughout the entire dorm. Joanne, Caleb's grandmother, and his aunt had driven to Morgantown for the party, and Joanne looked at me like she sensed something was wrong.

Later my own mother asked me, "Why didn't you say something to Joanne?"

I responded, "I couldn't have done that. She wouldn't have understood."

But Caleb's grandmother, the woman who had once told

me, "You'll find that we have a lot of skeletons in our closet," would have understood.

Joanne, more than anyone, liked to pretend that their family was perfect, but there was a darkness to the stories that other family members told me. The solution was never to try and help the person fix the behavior. The family closed ranks during a crisis. I couldn't have told Joanne without breaking that code. She would have called in the rest of the family, and they would have closed ranks against *me*.

THE BIRTHDAY PARTY was on Saturday, and although Caleb usually calmed down after a violent incident, I could sense that this time was different. The anger was not spent.

I HAD BEEN meeting Liz every week since I went to see her that first time. She suggested that Caleb and I write back and forth to each other in a notebook when we were angry rather than speaking to each other directly, but even those communications were disorienting.

I would write my feelings to him, and he would respond in a rage, yet a day later he would become apologetic, refuting everything that he had said during his rage.

Rage Caleb would write "Fuck off," but Apologetic Caleb would write "I don't deserve your forgiveness" and "You can't hold what I say when I'm angry against me. That's not what I mean."

Rage Caleb told me that he wasn't happy with me, Reed, his career, his family, or even the sun and weather.

Apologetic Caleb told me that he was ashamed of his be-havior and knew that he had messed up.

Apologetic Caleb told me that what he had done was un-forgivable, but asked for my forgiveness anyway.

I didn't even respond to his final letter, which was essen-tially begging.

I was so tired by then.

ON SUNDAY NIGHT, the day after Reed's party, I video-called Kelly M. when Caleb went to bed, and started sobbing. "He's so mean to me," I said. "He calls me terrible names. He screams at me all of the time. I'm scared of him." Even then, I didn't tell her that he hit me.

Kelly M. looked at me, her face horrified. "Oh, honey," she said. "That's not okay. It's not okay for him to treat you that way. I think that you need to leave him."

I knew that she was right, but I didn't think that I was ca-pable of leaving him. I didn't think that I would ever survive on my own. I finished the call, then curled up in bed next to Caleb, but I didn't wrap my arms around him this time, just turned my back.

ON MONDAY MORNING, I woke up angry. I had a T-shirt on, but had taken my underwear off during the night because it had kept crawling up my body and keeping me up.

Caleb had already taken Reed to the bus stop, and I went out to confront Caleb. He was eating cereal out of a heavy ceramic bowl. I told him that I had talked to Kelly M., and she had helped me realize that I needed to leave him. He screamed some things at me, and I turned to walk away. "Don't turn your butt to me!" he shouted, and because I was angry, I did a little flip of my bare butt at him. Then he threw the bowl at me. It shattered on my foot, and I fell to the ground, my body crashing into the milk and ceramic shards.

I knew that I was hurt badly.

I also knew that it wasn't over, and I had to hurry. I got up and hobbled to the bedroom, where I grabbed my phone. I had threatened to call 911 before, but Caleb had always taken my phone and broken it. He had probably broken three to four phones of mine a year.

He came into the room, and I told him, "I am going to call nine-one-one if you don't leave me alone."

"Call them, and tell them what a fucking bitch you are!"

And then I did it. I called. From that point on, everything changed.

CALEB ANSWERED THE door, and two campus police officers were there. The younger police officer took me into the back room while the older one talked to Caleb in the front. The first question the younger one asked me was, "Has this happened before?"

I cried and said "Yes," but that did not seem to be the answer that he was looking for. He told me, "It's all right. My wife and I fight. Things get crazy. Sometimes you just need time apart."

I nodded my head in agreement, but I wanted to ask, *Do you beat your wife too?*

The young policeman went out to the front room and told Caleb, "Go to your parents. Get away for a couple of days. Just let things calm down."

Caleb left, and the young policeman asked to see my driver's license, but when I stood up to get it, I found that I couldn't walk, that my foot was the size of a football, and it was bleeding. When the older policeman saw the swelling, the black and blue, and the toes like little sausage links, his expression turned to dismay. "That's bad. That looks broken," he said. "Ma'am, does your husband have a phone number we can reach him at? We need him to come back."

They waited outside, and I called Caleb. "I'm sorry," I said. "They are going to arrest you."

He said he already knew.

He left his phone on while they arrested him so that I could listen. I didn't want to, but I couldn't stop myself. "Did she hit you?" one of the officers asked—it was the older one, I think. "Because we can arrest her too."

Caleb answered honestly. He said no.

WHILE THE OLDER policeman arrested Caleb, the younger one waited with me for the paramedics to arrive. "Is he going to lose his job?" I asked.

"No, probably not," he said.

"Is he going to leave me?" I asked.

"You didn't do anything wrong," he said.

I wanted him to hug me so I could hide my face in the

folds of his black uniform. I crumpled into the rocking chair instead.

"He's going to leave me," I said.

The young policeman called for an ambulance. The EMTs looked at my foot. They didn't ask about what happened. They just told me it looked bad, that it could be broken. They asked me if I wanted to go to the emergency room, but I declined, so they instructed me to see a doctor and made me sign a waiver saying they weren't responsible if I didn't get follow-up care. And then I was alone in our house.

I called my mother, and I have no recollection of what she said. I then called Kelly M. and told her about the violence. After that, I called Megan and told her that Caleb had been beating me. I don't remember exactly what they said to me either, but I know that they both told me to *leave*.

Still, I stayed, and Caleb came home. The judge had let him go on his own recognizance and modified the no-contact order to a no-abusive-contact order, which meant that Caleb could come home to me as long as he didn't batter me. On his way home, he had called his parents and told them that he had been arrested for domestic battery. I don't know if what he relayed to me was true, but he said that he told them that it wasn't the first time and that he didn't want them to be angry with me. He said that Joanne told him to put our troubles at the "foot of the cross."

IT SEEMED THAT, with the exception of Kelly M. and Megan, no one thought that I was in actual danger, but I kept replaying incidents in my head.

The time that I had tried to fight back, and Caleb had held me down and spit in my face, not once, but four times.

The day that Caleb had told me that he needed to go to the mental hospital and check himself in. He needed to tell them that he wanted to murder his wife. I was terrified. I asked him why he would need to tell them that. I asked him, did he actually want to murder me?

The night that he pulled out my hair, then punched me in the spine with such force that my body arched back as though it had been shocked with electricity. I was jolted out of my cave. He did it again. "No!" I screamed. I could not protect myself.

My only protection was the darkness—the dissociation. I hadn't felt him ripping out hair, but when he hit me in the spine, the pain was too intense. That part of my body was too vulnerable. I couldn't curl up. I couldn't wrap my arms around it.

I was present for what was happening. I stopped breathing for a moment. He paused.

It was as though he, too, felt that I was present, and he stopped.

I knew I couldn't have been human to him in those moments.

I SPENT TWO days helping Caleb find a lawyer, trying to figure out how we were going to get his charges dismissed, and hoping that our marriage would change, but by then my mom had texted me in secret and made me promise that I would go to the domestic violence shelter. Kelly M. e-mailed me an escape plan that she had devised for me, and Megan, a counselor herself, helped me understand that things weren't going to change.

I lied and told Caleb that I was going to go grade papers, and then I went to see a counselor at the shelter. She described the cycle of abuse—tension building, battering incident, reconciliation, calm. It was so familiar. She explained to me that as the abuse escalated, we would spend less and less time in the calm stage, and more in the tension-building stage. She explained to me that the inevitable end to the cycle was death. My death.

I still downplayed my situation because I felt I didn't have the right to be taking up her time. "I'm sorry," I said. "You probably see women who are so much worse off. I realize that my situation isn't as bad as those other women's."

She looked at me in surprise, then said, "No, your situation is bad. It's really bad."

HE CHOKED ME once. Held his hands around my neck until the light around the edges of my eyes grew bright and foggy. While everything grew blurry for me, one thing remained in focus—his face in front of mine, his hands around my neck.

WHEN I RETURNED home, I didn't tell Caleb where I had been, but I picked up his iPad to search for something, and I saw that he had been looking at porn while I was gone. It hit me that I was the one doing all the work of trying to save a marriage that he was responsible for destroying.

I looked at him, and a chill went through my body. It was like my blood was turning thick, into ice. My fingers tingled. I knew I needed to leave.

A window opened.

And I jumped.

REED WAS AT day care, and I ran around the apartment, quickly grabbing as much as I could grab. Caleb followed me, screaming, "You are provoking me to abuse you." I got to the car, locked the doors, and drove off. I stopped at a gas station, and I followed the plan that Kelly M. had made for me. I called Rebecca, who was renting the house in Morgantown that Caleb and I owned. It wasn't an easy call to make.

I stood at that gas station, pumped gas, and talked to Rebecca on the phone. I asked her if Reed and I could stay with her for a while. The wind rushed between my ear and the phone, and after I hung up, I let the wind rush around me for a while before picking Reed up from day care.

We went to McDonald's for dinner, and I told Reed that we weren't going to be staying with Daddy for a while. He seemed unsurprised. We went back to Rebecca's and she set us up on the floor of the guest room. That night I curled up with Reed, and he asked me why we had to stay away from his daddy. I told him that it was because we couldn't get along, and we all needed some space to calm down. And then he told me, "I didn't like it when you and Daddy fought, because when you fought, you only had time for each other. You didn't have time for me." I hugged him and promised to always have time for him in the future.

The next day was Thursday, Thanksgiving Day. Caleb took Reed to his family's annual Thanksgiving dinner. While they ate turkey and dressing around the oak table I had eaten at so many times before, I returned to the apartment with Rebecca and threw as many things as I could fit into laundry baskets, then stuffed them into the back seat of my car. I packed Reed's Legos, enough blankets for us to sleep on the floor, and my work clothes, but I left behind anything sentimental. Our wedding photo was on a table, the glass broken. I had thrown it on the ground.

After packing, Rebecca and I ate at a Chinese buffet attached to a casino because it was the only place open in three counties.

ON FRIDAY, I hobbled around in denial for a few days until I had lunch with a friend. The first thing she said to me was, "You can apply for PhD programs now." The second thing she said to me was, "You need to get your foot examined."

I was embarrassed at the urgent care center. I told the nurse, "It's okay. He's already been arrested. I don't need anything. I'm safe," but he didn't seem to believe me. The nurse put me in a wheelchair even though I insisted I could walk, and the doctor touched and turned my foot with such care that, out of some sort of misguided impulse, I almost blurted out "Mom!" But I was thirty-four years old, and the distance between my mother and me was punctuated by so many mountains that she couldn't have saved me.

Liz had said to me, "You are taking everything he says, and playing it on repeat over and over again. You have to stop the tape."

But I couldn't stop the tape. Over and over I heard:

You are a fucking cunt. You are a fucking cunt. You are a fucking cunt. You are a fucking cunt. You are a fucking cunt. You are a fucking cunt. You are a fucking cunt.

And then his voice had become my voice:

I am a fucking cunt.

At the urgent care, the doctor said, "This will take a long time to heal. It will change color over time. It will look like a sunset." As I drove to Rebecca's, I heard the words over and over:

It will look like a sunset. It will look like a sunset. It will look like a sunset. It will look like a sunset. It will look like a sunset. It will look like a sunset. It will look like a sunset.

I knew that, this time, I had to be not just *leaving* him— but gone.

19

An Incomplete List of
Reasons He Was Violent

AFTER I LEFT Caleb, I started reading books, blogs, and websites. At night, in the darkness, when I lay awake in bed, one word rolled through my head on repeat. *Why?*

1. Maybe it was because of his family. His father hadn't abused his mother, but there were all of those supposed "skeletons" in the family. The stories I'd heard that were too shameful for me to even tell here. *Maybe that was what had caused Caleb's violence.*

2. Maybe it was because of Joanne. Maybe it was because of the way that Joanne seemed to *punish* Caleb when he didn't meet her standards. Maybe it was because of the way that Joanne treated Caleb like *the hero.* Maybe it was because Joanne seemed secretive. Maybe it was because Joanne did not seem secretive to protect herself, but to protect others. Maybe it was because Joanne cared too much about the ways in which the family was perceived. Maybe it was because I felt that Joanne used her love as a method of control. *Maybe that was what had caused Caleb's violence.*

3. Maybe it was because of Caleb's church. Maybe it was because the church was oppressive and guilt-based. Maybe it was because the preacher had scared Caleb when he was a child, had held snakes, and told the congregation that they were going to *burn in hell*. Maybe it had something to do with the story Caleb told me about the crush he had on that preacher's daughter, and that when the preacher noticed, he looked Caleb in the eye and told Caleb that he was not worthy of the preacher's daughter. *Maybe that was what had caused Caleb's violence.*

4. Maybe it was because of all the girls who rejected Caleb in high school. Caleb was already almost completely bald, and though he tried, he couldn't get a girlfriend. Maybe it was because of that one girl who had *treated him like shit and he wanted to fuck her.* That one girl who he did fuck when he was already with me. *Maybe that was what had caused Caleb's violence.*

5. Maybe it was because of Caleb's friends—the one who asked me if the *carpet matched the drapes.* The one who threw his fork at me and told me that it was my job to clean it up. The one who held on to his girlfriend's car while she was trying to drive away from him. Maybe it was because Caleb's friends didn't respect women, so why should he? *Maybe that was what had caused Caleb's violence.*

6. Maybe it was because of all the construction jobs that Caleb had held—the ways in which the men performed.

Maybe it was because of the guy who used to come up behind Caleb and fake-hump him. Maybe it was because Caleb had learned how to act *like a man* as a way of warding off the abuses of men like that. *Maybe that was what had caused Caleb's violence.*

7. Maybe it was because Caleb was hotheaded. Because he had been in too many fights to count. Maybe it was because Caleb had beat up a kid in middle school, and years later, Caleb's dad still bragged about how *proud* he was of Caleb for that. Maybe it was because Caleb had started a bar fight that had ended with his own head being cracked open. Maybe it was because Caleb and Cory had once gotten in a fistfight on a snowbank by the side of the road near Idaho City and almost tumbled off of a cliff. *Maybe that was what had caused Caleb's violence.*

8. Maybe it was because Caleb was disappointed in his career—in his inability to get published, in his failure to become a successful writer, in his lack of a tenure-track job. *Maybe that was what had caused Caleb's violence.*

9. Maybe it was because Caleb was disappointed by my career's success. *Maybe that was what had caused Caleb's violence.*

10. Maybe it was because of me. Maybe it was because I was inadequate, unworthy of his love. Maybe it was because I, too, was hotheaded. Maybe it was because of the time I fought back—that time that he held me down and spit in my face. Maybe it was because I never fully gave in. Maybe it was because I kept trying to stand up for

myself. Maybe it was because I, too, had changed during the marriage—had grown depressed, weepy, and angry. Maybe it was because I loved him in a desperate way, in a way that believed that we could return to the way that things had been in the beginning. Maybe it was because I had stopped believing that was possible. *Maybe I was what had caused Caleb's violence.*

Still, after all of my searching for answers, all I ever came up with was this: *Maybe it was time for me to stop wondering what had caused Caleb's violence and start focusing on my own healing.*

20

I Just Don't Know
What to Believe

A MONTH AFTER I left Caleb, Reed and I boarded an airplane by ourselves for the first time. He carried his own little backpack, but I carried everything else.

We had a layover in Minneapolis where we sat next to each other on the cold airport floor, my arm around Reed's shoulders, his body curled into my chest. There were families everywhere—fathers everywhere—and I was aware of the absence of my wedding ring on my hand. I was aware that, a year ago, I would have curled into Caleb's chest on the floor. I was aware that, a year ago, Caleb would have been the one who carried everything. I remembered Reed as a toddler crying, "Carry me. Carry me." I remembered how easy it had felt to carry him then.

When our flight was getting ready to board, the flight attendant called me to the front. "He is so cute," she said, nodding at Reed. "I've moved you up to first class." I wondered if my sadness had been visible. On the plane, the same flight attendant gave us a beverage and a packaged raspberry muffin. I had told Reed that first class was *fancy*. I was trying to be cheery about the fact that we would be spending our first Christmas without his father.

I unwrapped Reed's muffin and handed it to him. He took a bite and then closed his eyes and proclaimed loudly, "Mmm, this is the *best* muffin." He looked at me. "Isn't this the best muffin, Mommy? I don't think I've ever had a better muffin. First class has the best muffins."

I smiled and pushed his thick bangs away before leaning over to kiss his forehead. The flight attendant came back and surreptitiously set down three more muffins in front of Reed. He glowed, and I put them into my purse.

When we landed in Missoula, Montana, the woman who had been sitting behind us tapped Reed on the shoulder. "You were such a good boy," she said. "I collected all of the muffins that people weren't going to eat just for you." She handed him four more muffins, which I barely managed to fit in my purse. As we left the plane, Reed said, "Mommy, I was a good boy." He looked up at me, big blue eyes and red hair that reflected my own.

"Baby, you are always a good boy," I said.

When we saw my parents waiting in the arrivals area, we hugged, and I said, "Do you want some muffins?"

WE DROVE THREE hours, through the snow and over the Continental Divide, to make it to Salmon for Christmas. I don't remember what we talked about. I remember that the light refracting off the snow, and the blue skies that I had been yearning for, made my eyes hurt. I remember closing my eyes against all the pain.

THAT CHRISTMAS, I went to church with my parents. That Christmas, people asked me where Caleb was. That Christmas, I realized that my parents had not told anyone that I had left my husband. That Christmas, I made eye contact with everyone who asked and said calmly, "We have separated," while my mother winced and my father looked away.

That Christmas, while my father avoided me, my mother hovered. I spoke on the phone with a lawyer at West Virginia Legal Aid who, with a referral from the domestic violence shelter, would represent me for free if I could prove that my income was low enough and that the abuse was bad enough. She told me to bring any evidence of the abuse that I had, and I printed out e-mails from Caleb where he had admitted to hitting me. I used my parents' photo printer to print out photos of the bruises, of my swollen foot, of the damage done to the house, and I felt compelled to show it all to them.

My mother said to me, "Are you sure that this is what you want to do? Aren't you moving a little quickly?"

My father hadn't made eye contact with me in days.

WHEN REED AND I flew back to Morgantown, I arrived back at the house that Caleb and I owned. Rebecca had kindly moved out for me, so Reed and I no longer had to sleep on the floor. Caleb was living with his parents, and took Reed for a few days, so I set to unpacking. I was efficient—had nothing else to do, no friends or family nearby—so I unpacked the house within a day or two.

I wanted to make the bedroom that I had shared with Caleb my own, so I painted the floor black.

THEN I MET with the lawyer, Christine, a quiet, beautiful woman about my age. The first thing that she said was, "I have to ask this. Do you really want to leave him? I get clients here who are not ready to leave, and I need to know that you're ready."

I wasn't ready, but I knew that I was going to do it anyway, so I nodded. She looked at the evidence I had presented, and I felt foolish. "The abuse was probably not bad enough," I said. "And I'm probably not poor enough."

She looked at my tax statements. "You only made eighteen thousand last year," she said. "Our requirement is that you must have made under twenty-one thousand per year, so you meet the income guidelines." She got up and left the room to discuss the case with someone else, then came back and sat in front of me. "We have decided to take your case," she said.

I sat there quietly. All I could think was, I didn't imagine it. The abuse was real.

I WENT HOME and called Megan and Kelly M., who were both relieved that I was taking this step, and then I called my mother. She was hesitant but supportive.

I didn't talk to my father because we simply didn't talk anymore. Until we did.

I WAS HOME alone one evening, and Reed was in bed. I was cleaning my kitchen and talking to my father on the phone because he had answered while my mother was away, and I hadn't wanted to be rude and hang up. I was telling him details of the divorce, of my life. By then, because my friends had responded so supportively, I was pretty frank about the abuse. Still, my father was quiet. I stopped and said, "Dad, do you even believe me?"

"Kelly," he said, "I just don't know what to believe. It seems like you've always been a person who everything was going great for until it wasn't. Remember when you just up and moved to Portland? And then you just up and left Portland? Remember when you lived with your friend Kelly? And it was all fantastic, but then you suddenly had to move?"

WHEN MY FATHER told me that he "just didn't know what to believe," I felt the same ice in my hands that I felt when I left Caleb. "Dad, that Portland stuff happened fifteen years ago, and Kelly M. is still my best friend." He was silent. I don't think that he had even realized that the Kelly who was my best friend, who had introduced me to Caleb, *who was one of my bridesmaids*, was the same Kelly I had roomed with.

That was how little he knew about my life.

WHEN MY FATHER told me that he "just didn't know what to believe," I started sobbing. Wailing, in fact. I hung up on my father and called Megan.

"Honey," she said, "I can't understand a word you're saying. I'm going to need you to calm down enough for me to understand you, okay?"

And I calmed down enough to say, "My father just doesn't know what to believe."

WHEN MY FATHER told me that he "just didn't know what to believe," the truth was that I didn't know what to believe either. I knew that I was leaving Caleb by then, but I still loved him.

I wanted to say to my father, "Do you know how hard it is to leave someone you love?"

WHEN MY FATHER told me that he "just didn't know what to believe," there were days when I still wished that Caleb would beg me to take him back, promise to change, actually change.

Sometimes, when I was cooking dinner by myself, I could feel the way he would lay his head on my shoulder while I stirred a pot, the way he would turn me around and kiss me, tell me how much he loved my cooking, how beautiful I was, how lucky he was.

When my father told me that he "just didn't know what to believe," I fantasized about ways that Caleb and I could reunite. Still, I knew that, even if he never hit me again, my body would always remember that fist on my back.

WHEN MY FATHER told me that he "just didn't know what to believe," Megan took over for me. Her own mother's death had brought her closer to my parents, so my parents loved her. She was also a counselor, and she first e-mailed my parents articles and statistics, but when she didn't get a satisfactory response, Megan, the most nonconfrontational person I knew, picked up the phone, called my parents, and said, "You are going to lose your daughter if you can't support her in this."

WHEN MY FATHER told me that he "just didn't know what to believe," my mother called me. She said, "Your father wants to talk to you."

My father apologized, and he wept. My mother later told me that was the only time during their marriage that she had seen him cry. "He didn't even cry when his own mother died," she said.

I cried, too, but there was this new hardness in me that couldn't fully let my father, who had been my hero, back in. I thought of the man I had admired so much when I was growing up—the man who had worked so hard to protect the forests. I thought of how brave I had always considered him to be, and I thought, Why weren't you brave for me?

WHEN MY FATHER told me that he "just didn't know what to believe," I was an adjunct instructor teaching four classes, and I was still working in the dorm. When I signed on to teach four classes, my MFA thesis adviser had said, "Why would you take that many classes? You'll never be able to write."

I hedged. "I just think that I need to take as many classes as I can," I said. "In case things don't work out in the dorm."

He looked at me curiously. "Why wouldn't things work out?" he asked.

I ignored his question.

AFTER CALEB WAS arrested, the assistant provost came to visit us in the apartment. She told us that the university had a zero-tolerance policy on violence. It didn't take me long to realize that I was a part of that zero-tolerance policy, that she saw me as a participant rather than a victim. We were evicted, and she said that we would both be suspended with pay until the end of our terms.

But then she called me into her office. She said that, although Caleb would continue to get his pay, she couldn't really see any reason why I should continue to be paid.

I stared at her for a moment, then said, "You have no reason to fire me, and I am not quitting. I need this job to support my son. We live alone now." I hadn't realized that I had that much bravery until that moment.

She told me that she understood, but that I would need to think of some work that I could continue to do. I knew that she was bullying me, but I proposed some writing workshops and administrative work. All of it would require my presence in the dorm. She finally agreed, but she wanted me to go to meetings every Friday with the new resident faculty leaders and the hall director. They were meetings that wouldn't involve me at all and would be humiliating, but I told her that I would attend them. At the end of our appointment, I saw her look down at a note on her desk that had "$3,000" scrawled on it. She then said that, since my original contract had involved housing and food, she thought that she should give me a raise. She said that she would e-mail me an amount.

"That would be great," I said.

Then I stood up to leave, and she seemed to experience a moment of compassion. "Is that what he did to you?" she asked, nodding at the boot on my foot. Suddenly, it hurt. She saw my pain, but because she didn't want to know that pain, she turned her back to me, and I was *leaving* again.

SHE LATER E-MAILED me that they would give me an extra $1,000. I accepted it because I had already used up all of the fight that I had left in me.

WHEN MY FATHER told me that he "just didn't know what to believe," I went to the weekly meetings in the apartment where Caleb had been arrested for battering me, and I put on a smile, entertained students, and talked to the faculty, but I was always *leaving, leaving, leaving* because the minute that I walked into that apartment, I shivered in the same way that I had when I hid from Caleb in the closet.

WHEN MY FATHER told me that he "just didn't know what to believe," my professional outlook was not optimistic, and I knew that I needed to be Reed's primary caregiver. Once the dormitory job ended, I was going to have nothing. I had no money and no prospects. I didn't even have health insurance. West Virginia did not factor domestic violence against the mother into custody decisions, and the truth was that Caleb had never been abusive to Reed, so I was terrified that Caleb would get the primary custody he thought he should have.

And then, one morning, I got a phone call. I had been accepted to a PhD program in Ohio. I was still going to be poor, but I would have health coverage, and according to our pending divorce agreement, Reed was covered under Caleb's plan. I accepted.

CALEB HAD TOLD me that he was supportive of me getting the PhD. At one point he had even suggested moving to the same place as me so that he could continue to raise Reed as a coparent. He said, "You are going to be a grad student, but I have a stable job and life." I knew this was true, but I could not leave Reed with him.

I was terrified the court would make me stay in the state of West Virginia, and of losing Reed entirely to his father, so I gave Caleb almost everything that he wanted. I let him keep the house, which was our only asset. I let him have part of the summers with Reed. I let Caleb have everything that he wanted but me.

We had only one divorce hearing. My compromises were so great that the judge stopped the hearing in the middle and asked me, "Why are you doing this?"

I hadn't expected that question. "Because I want an agreement," I said.

The judge turned to Caleb. "Is that true?"

Caleb was flustered. He admitted to the judge that he had agreed not to create a legal battle for me if I gave him what he wanted. He told the judge that I would someday make more money than he would. His bitterness over this likelihood was apparent.

The judge was not pleased. He threw down his pen. He raised his voice. He said, "You should want your wife to be happy. What's best for your wife is what's best for your child."

But Caleb did not want what was best for me.

Caleb and I left the courthouse at the same time, but not together. Christine stayed by my side. I thought, Is she scared? I wasn't scared. I had stopped feeling fear long before that. The worst had already happened.

I thought I would cry in the car on the way home from my divorce. I even tried to muster up some tears. But they didn't come. Instead, I felt something in my chest. A weight released. And then, unexpectedly, euphoria. It was a euphoria stronger, even, than the dread I had felt on the eve of my wedding.

I was no longer *leaving*, but gone.

WHEN I ARRIVED at the house I had shared with Caleb, my parents were there to help me pack and move to Ohio. They expected me to be sad and broken, but that wasn't the case. I was happy—manic almost—and I set to bustling around the house and finishing the packing. My mother was obsessed with cleaning, as though I were moving out of a rental. I was dismissive, "Caleb can clean it," I said; he was moving back into the home where we had lived together. And as the day progressed, my father's mood darkened.

It was too easy for me, you see?

I had always been a flake, you see?

On the day of my divorce, my father and I had the worst fight of my life. He said, "Well, you also said that your mother abused you, and that wasn't true." I realized that my father still "just didn't know what to believe."

"I have never claimed that what Mom did to me was like what Caleb did to me," I said, feeling a rage inside me like I had never felt before.

I shouted at my father that I wanted him to leave.

My mother finally said, "Stop, this is not between you two." She looked into her lap. "You both need me to admit that something happened, and it did. I was not the best mother that I could have been, and I'm sorry."

I looked at my father for confirmation that he believed her—that he believed *me*—but he wouldn't look back at me.

"I want you to leave," I said again.

"Honey, no," my mother said. "You need us to help you."

"I don't need you anymore," I said, and I meant it. "I can do this on my own."

I looked at my father. "I forgive her because she couldn't help herself," I said, "but you were a coward."

AND THEN HE and my mother left. They got a hotel room for the night, but the next day, we all pretended that nothing had happened.

THE NEXT DAY, we went to dinner at a restaurant. I said something about the possibility of Reed having a stepparent someday. "I had a stepfather," my mother said. My father, who was driving, looked at her and said, "You never told me that."

"My mom married him after my father died," my mother said. "They were married for about a year before she died. He was so kind to me. He wanted to keep me and raise me, but my brother thought that it would be better if I went with him."

I was silent. I couldn't understand how my father and I had never known this before. I knew so little about my mother, about the grief that she must have felt when her parents died, about what her life had been like with her older brother as a surrogate parent. I thought about how much she had suffered in her life, how quietly she had accepted that suffering, and how I had followed that same pattern myself.

I no longer wanted to suffer quietly. I no longer wanted to be controlled by my story. I wanted to tell my story instead.

21

Goodbye, Sweet Girl

PEOPLE GO TO Motel 6 to die. Specifically, to the Motel 6 in Avoca, Iowa. But I hadn't come to Avoca to die. Like most patrons of Motel 6, I was on my way from somewhere to somewhere else, and I needed to sleep, but the ambulance lights flashing outside the double glass doors of the lobby weren't making me optimistic about my chances.

It had been nine months since I left Caleb. When summer arrived, my father flew out to meet me, and together we drove through the long, flattened heartland to the mountains of Idaho. I'd taken back my old summer job of working for the forest service, and I consoled myself with fantasies of rivers and snowcapped mountain peaks as I watched the Iowa sky listlessly pass me by. My father and I had four long days of driving together, and that time was what we needed.

WHEN I WAS in my early twenties, my father, my brother, and I drove to Kansas to see my grandmother. I had never spent time with my father without my mother, and as the mountains stretched into plains, my father and I talked quietly. For the first time, I grew to think of him as a friend.

After that, my father and I started backpacking together,

sometimes with my brother and sometimes just the two of us. We once backpacked into the Bob Marshall Wilderness in Montana together and climbed a tall mountain on the first day. At the summit, I could see the valleys covered in beargrass below me, and I felt so proud that I had conquered the ascent.

Years later, when I was in labor with Reed, I had cried out, "I can't do this."

My mother took my hand and said, "Yes, you can. Remember when you climbed into the Bob Marshall Wilderness with your father? He was so proud of you. He said that he'd had no idea that you were so strong, but you are strong, and you can do this."

And I did.

I remembered how I stopped backpacking with my father when I married Caleb.

I remembered how, by the end of our marriage, I didn't even drive. Caleb would drive me to work in the morning and pick me up in the evenings. It was control disguised as help. He drove me everywhere to such an extent that I had grown fearful of driving myself, but there I was, hands on the steering wheel, my father in the passenger seat, navigating the turnpikes around Chicago. "I'm glad that you're the one driving," he said. "This is a real mess." He didn't know how scared I had been to drive, but he knew enough to be proud of me.

My father had always wanted what was best for me. He just didn't necessarily know what that thing was. I was still hurt that he hadn't believed me, but I came to realize that my well-being was my own responsibility, and that I needed to learn how to take care of myself.

MY TEACHING CONTRACT in West Virginia had ended in May, and I was moving to Ohio in August. Our custody arrangement gave Caleb six weeks in the summer with Reed, and I was at a loss for how to fill the time. It seemed fitting somehow to retreat to the wilderness.

Once back in Idaho, I lived and worked in an A-frame at the end of a long dirt road. Perched just before the Frank Church River of No Return Wilderness border, my A-frame was at the base of tall black-rock cliffs that cradled the Salmon River, a river so deep in places that prehistoric fish could survive for a hundred years in dark pools. It is one of the last places in the world where the stars are undimmed by electric lights.

I remembered how much fun I had in my twenties when I worked there with my friend Jen. Back then, surrounded by good-looking river guides and outdoorsmen, we had had a lot of sexy fun, and though a lot had changed since then, Jen still worked for the forest service. When I called to tell her that I was leaving Caleb, she said, "Come home." So I did.

JEN SCHEDULED ME to work with Emily, a tanned woman with a bleached blond pixie cut, a collection of hooded sweatshirts, a foul mouth, and a laugh that I could hear from across a room. On the surface, we seemed to have nothing in common. Still, like me, Emily was sad, and I loved her immediately.

A few months earlier, Emily's husband's twin brother had died in his sleep of an aneuryom. Emily met her husband when she was only sixteen, and her brother-in-law had lived with them for years. He was as close to her as a biological brother, and although she was brassy and funny in a tough-shelled way, when she fell silent—which was rare—I always knew what she was thinking.

AS EMILY DESCRIBED the loss of her brother-in-law, I knew that I had been lucky. Caleb was still breathing, still alive. Leaving him had been like giving up a drug. I had to white-knuckle through the nights without him, but I had made the decision. I had taken control.

Emily and Jen decided that the cure for my sadness would be to get laid. Together, we mulled over my prospects among this new batch of river guides and outdoorsmen. Yoga Dude was a former river guide turned ranger, and he and I shared a tiny A-frame as part of our living arrangement. On a river trip, Jen, Emily, and I reclined in beach chairs with beers while he took his shirt off and stretched on the beach.

"He does have a good body," Jen said, taking a sip of Coors Lite.

"Yeah, but he likes to rescue bugs," I said. "He catches them and releases them outside."

"And he's always talking about what a 'nice guy' he is,"

said Emily. "No one who is truly a 'nice guy' ever refers to himself that way."

A month later, Yoga Dude snuck into my bedroom in the A-frame and stole the spider traps that Jen had set up for me before I moved in. I only realized that Yoga Dude had removed the traps when I brought Emily into my room to kill a black widow for me. It disappeared before she could get it, and I couldn't sleep for a week.

"I don't like Yoga Dude," I said. "He can keep his Buddhism to himself."

THEN THERE WAS Burly Guy, a brawny, cheerful man who still remembered me from a decade earlier. Burly Guy was a rent-a-guide, which meant he would work for any river company who would have him. Most likely, this attitude extended to his personal relationships.

"He was flirting with you. And he remembers you," Emily said. "You should totally sleep with Burly Guy."

"Well, he is cute," I said. "And he's so huge that he makes me feel petite."

We speculated about how we could make this coupling happen. We finally settled on me just approaching him and saying, "Wanna go?" while cocking my head toward the A-frame.

But when Burly Guy came back the following week, Emily pushed me to actually approach him, and I just couldn't.

"I don't think I'm ready," I said. "I don't think I want to be with anyone else."

"Kell," she said, her face kind, "I didn't mean to pressure you. I just thought it was what you wanted."

I didn't know how to tell her that my true desire was not to be with someone else, but to *want* to be with someone else, and worse, that I still missed Caleb every moment.

EMILY WAS RELIGIOUS and thought that God had brought us into each other's lives, and though I had lost the religion of my childhood, I almost believed her. I had felt so alone before I lived with her that summer. Together, we were united by grief. In a dream she had, her husband's twin appeared and told her not to be sad anymore, that everything was going to be okay.

"The dream was so vivid," she said, starting to cry. "It was as real as if he was there with me. I think it was his spirit."

"Oh, Em. I'm sure it was," I said. What I didn't tell her was that sometimes Caleb appeared in my dreams—as real as though he was in the room with me—and sometimes he, too, told me not to be sad anymore, that everything was going to be okay. But Caleb was alive, watching our son alone across the country. It wasn't Caleb's spirit that comforted me in my dreams. It was the ghost of the man I had wanted him to be. When I woke from those dreams, I didn't feel that everything was going to be okay. Instead, I wanted to close my eyes and go back to the dream.

EVEN THOUGH I knew I wasn't ready to be with someone else, Emily, Jen, and I still joked about the different men I could have sex with. It was fun being crass and made me feel normal again. The best option was probably Bearded Man, another rent-a-guide. He knew Emily and Jen from the river, and I used to casually date him.

"Whaaaat?" Emily shrieked when I told her we had dated years before. "What happened?"

"It was long-distance and wasn't going to work, and then I met Caleb."

"Kelly says that Bearded Man is really good in bed," Jen interrupted me, saying what I had said with a wink.

I remembered long, athletic afternoons with Bearded Man. He had a physicality about him that appealed to me. We'd put on a Prince album, and Prince would finish before we did.

"It's going to be Bearded Man!" Emily said.

And it was.

I didn't plan it, but it happened.

HAVING SEX WITH someone after almost a decade of marriage was a bit like losing my virginity again. I thought I had accumulated a lot of knowledge throughout my marriage, but it turned out to be particular to the two us. Bearded Man and I no longer knew each other's bodies as we had the first summer we were together.

Still, as with losing my virginity, there was a part of me that was just glad to have it out of the way. And I did feel better. The sex abated my sadness a bit, and I thought of Caleb a little less often.

But having sex with Bearded Man couldn't take away the memories of my time with Caleb. At its best, sex with Caleb was like being in a snow globe together, protected by a glass bubble that contained only magic and no trouble. Shortly before I left him, I said to Caleb, "I'll never love anyone but you." It sounds tinny and hollow in my memory, but at the time I meant it as both a promise and a plea.

BEARDED MAN AND I saw each other a few more times, and the sex got better, but then I had to leave. My chest deflated when we hugged, but I was also relieved. I still loved Caleb, and after all, things hadn't worked out with Bearded Man the first time. It was good that I was leaving.

IN AUGUST I packed up my car and started the long solo drive from Idaho to West Virginia; I was no longer afraid of driving. I was going to pick up Reed and then move to Ohio. My chest constricted as I drove through the Badlands of South Dakota. The absence of the mountains felt like a physical loss, and when I stopped along the way at the Motel 6 in Avoca, Iowa, I wondered if I was making the wrong decision. I checked in and saw my dining options, which consisted of a Taco John's attached to a gas station and an Iowa chain that specialized in some sort of "meat sandwich." I missed Emily and Jen, the river, and Caleb, most of all.

Still, none of that kept my dog from needing a walk. I had kept the smaller dog because I was going to have to rent an apartment in my PhD program, and Caleb had kept our larger dog because of his yard. Losing the first dog that Caleb and I had adopted together had been yet another loss, but I was grateful for the dog I had. As I walked him down the hall on his leash, I saw a door propped open with a trash can. The room was in disarray. The covers lay on the floor, and white-sock-clad feet poked off the edge of the bed. A couple of paramedics pushed by me with a stretcher.

"What happened?" I asked the night clerk in the lobby.

"Someone just OD'd," she said with a shrug, as though people regularly committed suicide at the Avoca Motel 6.

I walked my dog out to a patch of grass, the din of vehicles on the interstate rushing by. The sun was setting, and the Iowa sky—so large—loomed in front of me. Nearly the same red and blue as the color of the ambulance lights swept across the skyline, and it was so heartbreakingly beautiful and at the same time so much like a bruise that I broke down crying in that parking lot. A trucker who had been working on his truck scurried off when I started sobbing.

A couple of years earlier, one of my high school friends had lost both her husband and child in a tragic car accident. Later Jeannie sent me a Facebook message and told me to look up "Orchid Leona Sun."

I typed in the name and saw the face of my friend, who now had blond hair instead of the brown hair I remembered her having in high school. She'd begun wearing hippie dresses, and she was a midwife. From what I could gather, she had completely changed her name and her life.

"She seems happy," I said when Jeannie asked me what I thought of the change.

Jeannie, who was a counselor, hesitated before replying. "I don't think it's good," she finally said. "I mean, wherever you go, there you are. You can't escape your past." She was right. Our friend had changed her name, her dress, her job, and what seemed like her whole damn life, but there would always be a part of her that was still the person I went to high school with, still the person with brown hair who remembered her lost husband and child, and grieved for them.

Wherever I went, there I was. There I was. There I was. There I was.

SHORTLY BEFORE I left Idaho in August, Emily and I went down to a beach where we put little floating chairs in the water and watched the sun set together. We talked as though we would never run out of things to say. It was our last night together, and our speech was urgent, as if we knew that we could never return to that moment, to the newness of our friendship, to the magic of that connection, to the commonality of our grief.

I told her about the first night that I saw Bearded Man again, how I sat with him on a dock and looked at the stars. "I don't remember the last time I saw the Big Dipper," I told him. "I'm not sure why I stopped looking at the stars."

He had snorted in disbelief, and I realized how much of myself I had lost in the years of my marriage.

Emily told me about her family, her parents' divorce and

her quiet suffering, her love for her brother-in-law and her worry that she hadn't been good enough to him while he was alive. She also told me about her feeling that he forgave her. That he was always watching over her with love.

I told her that I didn't miss Caleb anymore, at least not all of the time. "I was like an open wound when I got here," I said.

"You're a completely different person now than you were when you arrived," she said. She paused, and then spoke again. "My husband asked me if I've told you how much you mean to me right now. You've been so important to me this summer. I just want you to know."

"I know," I said.

I sat next to her, floating in the water, watching the sun dip behind the canyon, and I tried memorizing everything about that moment. I wanted to always remember the cool dark water of the Salmon River, the warm sand, the smell of pine, the sky so large, canopied with stars. It was the first time that I felt that I could be happy again. Caleb was no-where nearby, and he never would be again, but my friend was there. And I was there.

WHEN I WAS in the fourth grade, my teacher chartered a small plane. So many Idahoans, she said, would never get a chance to ride an airplane. I was thrilled as I boarded the plane. I was the lucky one to ride in the front seat. As we rose into the air, the pilot made a large sweep over the valley, the tiny houses receding into the distance, the dark river slicing through green pastures, flanked by steep mountains. I knew that I would never be the same as I glided in that immensity. It was as though I could see the girl who I had been standing in that valley, waving furiously back at me. Goodbye, sweet girl, I thought.

Eight years later, when I had dropped out of college and was flying to Europe, I looked down into the shadowy depths of the ocean and thought I saw myself reflected in the water. Five years after that, I gripped the door handle of a two-seater as it sliced up the stark Salmon River canyon and dropped me off at a tiny dirt airstrip at Indian Creek. As the plane flew away, and I prepared myself to spend weeks alone in the wilderness for the first time, it was as though I could see the girl I had been flying away in that plane.

Five years after that, I flew with Reed and Joanne to my new home in West Virginia, where I was meeting Caleb, and as the Idaho skyline disappeared behind me into vast reaches of blue, I could see myself disappearing too.

Now, six years later, I stood staring at that wide, open Iowa sky, surrounded by nothing but chain restaurants, a potential suicide, and a funeral home. An airplane streaked by, leaving a white tail in its wake. I thought about sitting by the river with Emily and savored the details I had willed myself to remember. I saw the bruised woman who I had been cradled in that cool water, still recovering from her Caleb life. But now I saw her as a memory, and I could finally say to her, "Goodbye, sweet girl."

Epilogue
The House in the Hollow

WHEN WE ARRIVED in Ohio, Reed and I first moved into a sterile apartment run by student housing. I carried my groceries up six flights of metal stairs. I carried my dog down the stairs to go potty when the steps were too cold for his paws.

I missed Reed desperately when he was away at school or visiting his dad.

Still, when we moved into that tiny apartment, Reed and I found a cute little blue table that we fit around perfectly.

And slowly, I found beauty in this town.

A YEAR LATER, I found a little house in the hollow. It's a tiny house, but it has skylights that let rainbows of light inside, and a loft office where I can write and Reed can call up to me when he needs me. We are surrounded by woods—thick green trees that change color in the autumn—and my father, the forester, gasped when he saw the beautiful English maple in the yard. Our neighbors are kind, and my landlord, who lives behind us, plays soccer outside with his own son and Reed.

It hasn't been easy, and I'm tired, but I'm tired because I'm getting better. I'm tired because my heart is no longer a tight little fist that can't even recognize it's lonely. I don't want my heart to be a tight little fist. I want my heart to be an open hand, reaching out.

THERE WAS A day when I was home for Christmas, and Reed, my mom, and I were making sugar cookies. I rolled out the dough. "I'm grateful that Reed isn't like I was when I was a kid," I said. "He's such a great kid."

My mom looked up in surprise. "You were a great kid," she said.

I was confused. "But I was always in trouble," I said.

"Sure," she said, "but just for stuff like not cleaning your room. You never lied, and you were never mean. You were so kind to other children. Your father and I always knew that you were a good kid."

I stood there, an adult—on the other side of a kitchen island from my aging mother—and the distance between us suddenly lessened.

I wanted to say, *Why did it take you so long to tell me this?*

I wanted to say, *Thank you.*

But I said nothing and rolled out a cookie instead. I handed a sugary Santa to Reed. "Everyone says that I'm a lot like my mom," he said as he stretched the cold dough out on the baking sheet.

THERE WAS ANOTHER day when my mother followed me into the laundry room at her house. She hugged me and said, "We know how much you've been through, and we are so proud of you and who you have become." I broke down into tears then, and this time I said it: "Thank you, Mama."

I remembered that night before my wedding shower when my mother and I walked in the dark canyon with the howling wolves. She hadn't seemed scared at all, but I was terrified. I was scared of that night, of my future, of those wolves, of spending the night in a car the day before I met my future in-laws for the first time, of being married, and most of all, of the child in my womb. I wasn't ready for any of it, but she took my arm and guided me back to that car. My mother was tough. If the wolves had circled us then, she would have stared them down, but I would have run.

BUT NOW? NOW, I would stare down the wolves too. Writing is my way of staring down the wolves.

I STARTED RUNNING on the treadmill after I left Caleb. I was trying to create enough physical pain to obliterate the emotional pain. A pop song came on, the lyrics saying, "What doesn't kill you only makes you stronger."

I thought, I am not stronger. I am not stronger because of what he did to me.

But I am stronger. And I was strong before I met him. And I was strong during the abuse.

IT WAS MY strength that gave me the integrity to try and do what I thought was best for our child, who loved his father, even though I was suffering personally. It was my strength that told me to make the demands that I did make: that he would need to get counseling, that he would need to quit drinking, that he would need to go to anger management, that he would need to take medication. It was my strength that made me adaptable enough to survive while he tried these different strategies. It was my strength that made me eventually realize that these strategies were not going to work. And it was my ultimate strength when I gave up.

I still run on the treadmill, but now I enjoy it. The other night I went to pick Reed up from my landlord's house. I didn't realize that Reed had run over there in his bare feet. It was getting late, and the ground was getting cold, so I gave him a piggyback ride home. He said, "Even my dad can't carry me on his back anymore."

He said, "Mom, you are getting so strong."

I STILL HAVE that blue table in our little house in the hollow, and Reed and I still fit perfectly at that table, but we also share that table now with our many friends.

Spring in the new home is beautiful. The hum of the bugs. The moan of the toads. The rain on the skylights. We moved into this home in spring, and on our first day here, Reed and I swung together in the hammock in the backyard.

Reed curled up next to me and said, "Everything is just better now, isn't it?"

Acknowledgments

Thank you to my editor Gail Winston who has tirelessly supported me through each stage of this book. I am grateful for her keen editorial eye, but also for her kind heart. This was a difficult book to write, and I could not have asked for a better editor to navigate me through this process.

Thank you to my agent, Joy Tutela. Like Gail, she has guided me with kindness, and I feel fortunate to consider her not only my best professional ally but also a generous and thoughtful friend. Thank you, also, to Susan Raihoffer, foreign rights agent extraordinaire.

Thank you to everyone at HarperCollins who has touched this book in some way—Sofia Groopman, Mary Gaule, Susan Amster, Miranda Otewell, and anyone else I may have forgotten.

Thank you to my mentors Dinty W. Moore and Kevin Oderman. Good men are out there, and I know this because of them.

Thank you to the generous faculty members and educators who nurtured this project and helped me to grow as a writer: Mark Brazaitis, Eric LeMay, Ghirmai Negash, and Joan Connor.

Thank you to Helen Bertram for telling a shy, awkward, and insecure teenager that she could be a writer.

Thank you to Rebecca Solnit for telling a shy, awkward, and insecure adult that she could be a writer.

Thank you to my fairy godsisters who have supported or shared my work in some way: Barbara Jones, Katherine Dykstra, Lisa Lucas, Melanie Bishop, Ariel Levy, Roxane Gay, Ashley Cassandra Ford, Christa Parravani, Megan Stielstra, Amy Butcher, Maggie Smith, Lisa Nikolidakis, Mo Daviau, Rene Denfeld, Cheryl Strayed, Lindy West, and so many others. None of this would have been possible without the support of other women writers, editors, and publishers, and I am so grateful.

Thank you to Michael Archer, Hillary Brenhouse, Rachel Riederer, and all of the good people at *Guernica* magazine. You're family to me now.

Thank you to Celia Blue Johnson and Maria Gagliano at *Slice* magazine. You launched my career, and you've generously become my friends.

Thank you to the many first-readers of this (or parts of this) manuscript, particularly Todd Gleason, Jenny Respress, Heather Frese-Sanchez, Rebecca Schwab-Cuthbert, Keema Waterfield, Christian Exoo, Patri Thompson, Shane Stricker, and others.

Thank you to the people who gave me the space and/or funding to make this book possible: Dickinson House Writer's Residency, Rebecca Solnit, Karen and Doug Sholes, Vermont Studio Center, The Mineral School, The National Endowment for the Arts, Ohio University, Oddfellows Bakery, and the Village Bakery.

Thank you to my therapist, Liz Gilchrist, who I called

on the day that I left Caleb. I told her that I had left Caleb, and she said, "I am going to treat you for free for a while. I don't want you to stop seeing me because you're worried about money." Liz hasn't charged me since, but she has been there whenever I've needed her. Every day, I'm overwhelmed with the generosity of others, and Liz is a pioneer in generosity.

Thank you to Christine Schneider from West Virginia Legal Aid. Without her help, I might never have left the state, and I might never have escaped.

Oh goodness, how to thank my friends? I have been blessed with so many good and steadfast friends, and I couldn't possibly name them all here, so I have decided not to name any of them. If you're reading this, and you're my friend, please know that I appreciate you, and your name is written on this page in invisible ink.

It takes a village to raise a child, and this is even truer for single parents. Thank you to my Athens village, particularly Erin Perko, Mary Kate Hurley, Alison Stine, and Renita Romasco.

Thank you to my best friend and my brother, Glen. I'm sorry that I ruined your Christmas when I was born, but I hope that I've been making your days better ever since.

Thank you to my parents who have lovingly grown with me throughout this process. I know that this book was not easy on them, and I know that the process of me writing this book was not easy on them, but their kindness, fairness, and genuine love for Reed and me has made all of this possible, and I will never forget that.

Finally—though he is not allowed to read this book until he's older—thank you to my son, Reed. My favorite person. My silly tween who makes me laugh. My boy who is so proud that his mama wrote a book. My boy who let me write on Saturdays and snow days. My boy who said, "You should just let me read your book because I pretty much know it all already." My boy who was wrong about that, but who knows enough about what's in these pages that I've never struggled with whether I should write this book or not.

My boy who once said to me, "I'm glad that you left my dad because you are so nice, and I don't know if I ever would have gotten to know your niceness when my dad was around."

Single parenting is hard, but single parenting a child like Reed is easy. He is the best thing that has ever happened to me. I will not say that I'm grateful for what Caleb did to me, but what I will say is that I would do it all again if I ended up in this exact place again—Reed and me sitting on the couch laughing, eating dinner, and watching *Bob's Burgers*.

I jumped, I took him with me, and I've never regretted that decision.

To all of the women out there who are thinking about leaving, *do it*.

Jump.

About the Author

Kerry Conberg's essays have appeared in *Guernica, Gulf Coast, The Rumpus, Denver Quarterly, Slice,* and others. Her essay "It Will Look Like a Sunset" was selected for inclusion in *The Best American Essays 2015,* and other essays have been listed as notables in the same series. She has a PhD in creative nonfiction from Ohio University and has been the recipient of fellowships or grants from Vermont Studio Center, A Room of Her Own Foundation, Dickinson House, and the National Endowment for the Arts.